THE TEMPEST

William Shakespeare

Spark Publishing
A Division of Barnes & Noble
120 Fifth Avenue
New York, NY 10011
www.sparknotes.com

ISBN-13: 978-1-5866-3412-4
ISBN-10: 1-5866-3412-7

Library of Congress information available upon request.

Please submit changes or report errors to www.sparknotes.com/errors.

Printed and bound in the United States.

1 3 5 7 9 10 8 6 4 2

A PROLOGUE FROM THE BARD

Brave scholars, blessed with time and energy,
    At school, fair Harvard, set about to glean,
From dusty tomes and modern poetry,
    All truths and knowledge formerly unseen.
From forth the hungry minds of these good folk
    Study guides, star-floss'd, soon came to life;
Whose deep and deft analysis awoke
    The latent "A"s of those in lit'rary strife.
Aim far past passing—insight from our trove
    Will free your comprehension from its cage.
Our SparkNotes' worth, online we also prove;
    Behold this book! Same brains, but paper page.
If patient or "whatever," please attend,
    What you have missed, our toil shall strive to mend.

CONTENTS

CONTEXT

THE MOST INFLUENTIAL WRITER in all of English literature, William Shakespeare was born in 1564 to a successful middle-class glove-maker in Stratford-upon-Avon, England. Shakespeare attended grammar school, but his formal education proceeded no further. In 1582 he married an older woman, Anne Hathaway, and had three children with her. Around 1590 he left his family behind and traveled to London to work as an actor and playwright. Public and critical acclaim quickly followed, and Shakespeare eventually became the most popular playwright in England and a part-owner of the Globe Theater. His career bridged the reigns of Elizabeth I (ruled 1558–1603) and James I (ruled 1603–1625), and he was a favorite of both monarchs. Indeed, James granted Shakespeare's company the greatest possible compliment by bestowing upon its members the title of King's Men. Wealthy and renowned, Shakespeare retired to Stratford and died in 1616 at the age of fifty-two. At the time of Shakespeare's death, literary luminaries such as Ben Jonson hailed his works as timeless.

Shakespeare's works were collected and printed in various editions in the century following his death, and by the early eighteenth century his reputation as the greatest poet ever to write in English was well established. The unprecedented admiration garnered by his works led to a fierce curiosity about Shakespeare's life, but the dearth of biographical information has left many details of Shakespeare's personal history shrouded in mystery. Some people have concluded from this fact and from Shakespeare's modest education that Shakespeare's plays were actually written by someone else—Francis Bacon and the Earl of Oxford are the two most popular candidates—but the support for this claim is overwhelmingly circumstantial, and the theory is not taken seriously by many scholars.

In the absence of credible evidence to the contrary, Shakespeare must be viewed as the author of the thirty-seven plays and 154 sonnets that bear his name. The legacy of this body of work is immense. A number of Shakespeare's plays seem to have transcended even the category of brilliance, becoming so influential as to affect profoundly the course of Western literature and culture ever after.

The Tempest probably was written in 1610–1611, and was first performed at Court by the King's Men in the fall of 1611. It was performed again in the winter of 1612–1613 during the festivities in celebration of the marriage of King James's daughter Elizabeth. *The Tempest* is most likely the last play written entirely by Shakespeare, and it is remarkable for being one of only two plays by Shakespeare (the other being *Love's Labor's Lost*) whose plot is entirely original. The play does, however, draw on travel literature of its time—most notably the accounts of a tempest off the Bermudas that separated and nearly wrecked a fleet of colonial ships sailing from Plymouth to Virginia. The English colonial project seems to be on Shakespeare's mind throughout *The Tempest,* as almost every character, from the lord Gonzalo to the drunk Stefano, ponders how he would rule the island on which the play is set if he were its king. Shakespeare seems also to have drawn on Montaigne's essay "Of the Cannibals," which was translated into English in 1603. The name of Prospero's servant-monster, Caliban, seems to be an anagram or derivative of "Cannibal."

The extraordinary flexibility of Shakespeare's stage is given particular prominence in *The Tempest.* Stages of the Elizabethan and Jacobean period were for the most part bare and simple. There was little on-stage scenery, and the possibilities for artificial lighting were limited. The King's Men in 1612 were performing both at the outdoor Globe Theatre and the indoor Blackfriars Theatre and their plays would have had to work in either venue. Therefore, much dramatic effect was left up to the minds of the audience. We see a particularly good example of this in *The Tempest,* Act II, scene i when Gonzalo, Sebastian, and Antonio argue whether the island is beautiful or barren. The bareness of the stage would have allowed either option to be possible in the audience's mind at any given moment.

At the same time, *The Tempest* includes stage directions for a number of elaborate special effects. The many pageants and songs accompanied by ornately costumed figures or stage-magic—for example, the banquet in Act III, scene iii, or the wedding celebration for Ferdinand and Miranda in Act IV, scene i—give the play the feeling of a masque, a highly stylized form of dramatic, musical entertainment popular among the aristocracy of the sixteenth and seventeenth centuries. It is perhaps the tension between simple stage effects and very elaborate and surprising ones that gives the play its eerie and dreamlike quality, making it seem rich and complex even though it is one of Shakespeare's shortest, most simply constructed plays.

It is tempting to think of *The Tempest* as Shakespeare's farewell to the stage because of its theme of a great magician giving up his art. Indeed, we can interpret Prospero's reference to the dissolution of "the great globe itself" (IV.i.153) as an allusion to Shakespeare's theatre. However, Shakespeare is known to have collaborated on at least two other plays after *The Tempest*: *The Two Noble Kinsmen* and *Henry VIII* in 1613, both probably written with John Fletcher. A performance of the latter was, in fact, the occasion for the actual dissolution of the Globe. A cannon fired during the performance accidentally ignited the thatch, and the theater burned to the ground.

CONTEXT

PLOT OVERVIEW

A STORM STRIKES A SHIP carrying Alonso, Ferdinand, Sebastian, Antonio, Gonzalo, Stefano, and Trinculo, who are on their way to Italy after coming from the wedding of Alonso's daughter, Claribel, to the prince of Tunis in Africa. The royal party and the other mariners, with the exception of the unflappable Boatswain, begin to fear for their lives. Lightning cracks, and the mariners cry that the ship has been hit. Everyone prepares to sink.

The next scene begins much more quietly. Miranda and Prospero stand on the shore of their island, looking out to sea at the recent shipwreck. Miranda asks her father to do anything he can to help the poor souls in the ship. Prospero assures her that everything is all right and then informs her that it is time she learned more about herself and her past. He reveals to her that he orchestrated the shipwreck and tells her the lengthy story of her past, a story he has often started to tell her before but never finished. The story goes that Prospero was the Duke of Milan until his brother Antonio, conspiring with Alonso, the King of Naples, usurped his position. With the help of Gonzalo, Prospero was able to escape with his daughter and with the books that are the source of his magic and power. Prospero and his daughter arrived on the island where they remain now and have been for twelve years. Only now, Prospero says, has Fortune at last sent his enemies his way, and he has raised the tempest in order to make things right with them once and for all.

After telling this story, Prospero charms Miranda to sleep and then calls forth his familiar spirit Ariel, his chief magical agent. Prospero and Ariel's discussion reveals that Ariel brought the tempest upon the ship and set fire to the mast. He then made sure that everyone got safely to the island, though they are now separated from each other into small groups. Ariel, who is a captive servant to Prospero, reminds his master that he has promised Ariel freedom a year early if he performs tasks such as these without complaint. Prospero chastises Ariel for protesting and reminds him of the horrible fate from which he was rescued. Before Prospero came to the island, a witch named Sycorax imprisoned Ariel in a tree. Sycorax died, leaving Ariel trapped until Prospero arrived and freed him. After Ariel assures Prospero that he knows his

5

place, Prospero orders Ariel to take the shape of a sea nymph and make himself invisible to all but Prospero.

Miranda awakens from her sleep, and she and Prospero go to visit Caliban, Prospero's servant and the son of the dead Sycorax. Caliban curses Prospero, and Prospero and Miranda berate him for being ungrateful for what they have given and taught him. Prospero sends Caliban to fetch firewood. Ariel, invisible, enters playing music and leading in the awed Ferdinand. Miranda and Ferdinand are immediately smitten with each other. He is the only man Miranda has ever seen, besides Caliban and her father. Prospero is happy to see that his plan for his daughter's future marriage is working, but decides that he must upset things temporarily in order to prevent their relationship from developing too quickly. He accuses Ferdinand of merely pretending to be the Prince of Naples and threatens him with imprisonment. When Ferdinand draws his sword, Prospero charms him and leads him off to prison, ignoring Miranda's cries for mercy. He then sends Ariel on another mysterious mission.

On another part of the island, Alonso, Sebastian, Antonio, Gonzalo, and other miscellaneous lords give thanks for their safety but worry about the fate of Ferdinand. Alonso says that he wishes he never had married his daughter to the prince of Tunis because if he had not made this journey, his son would still be alive. Gonzalo tries to maintain high spirits by discussing the beauty of the island, but his remarks are undercut by the sarcastic sourness of Antonio and Sebastian. Ariel appears, invisible, and plays music that puts all but Sebastian and Antonio to sleep. These two then begin to discuss the possible advantages of killing their sleeping companions. Antonio persuades Sebastian that the latter will become ruler of Naples if they kill Alonso. Claribel, who would be the next heir if Ferdinand were indeed dead, is too far away to be able to claim her right. Sebastian is convinced, and the two are about to stab the sleeping men when Ariel causes Gonzalo to wake with a shout. Everyone wakes up, and Antonio and Sebastian concoct a ridiculous story about having drawn their swords to protect the king from lions. Ariel goes back to Prospero while Alonso and his party continue to search for Ferdinand.

Caliban, meanwhile, is hauling wood for Prospero when he sees Trinculo and thinks he is a spirit sent by Prospero to torment him. He lies down and hides under his cloak. A storm is brewing, and Trinculo, curious about but undeterred by Caliban's strange appearance and smell, crawls under the cloak with him. Stefano, drunk and singing, comes along and stumbles upon the bizarre spectacle of Caliban and Trinculo huddled under the cloak. Caliban, hearing the singing, cries out that he will work faster so long as the "spirits" leave him alone. Stefano decides that this monster requires liquor and attempts to get Caliban to drink. Trinculo recognizes his friend Stefano and calls out to him. Soon the three are sitting up together and drinking. Caliban quickly becomes an enthusiastic drinker, and begins to sing.

Prospero puts Ferdinand to work hauling wood. Ferdinand finds his labor pleasant because it is for Miranda's sake. Miranda, thinking that her father is asleep, tells Ferdinand to take a break. The two flirt with one another. Miranda proposes marriage, and Ferdinand accepts. Prospero has been on stage most of the time, unseen, and he is pleased with this development.

Stefano, Trinculo, and Caliban are now drunk and raucous and are made all the more so by Ariel, who comes to them invisibly and provokes them to fight with one another by impersonating their voices and taunting them. Caliban grows more and more fervent in his boasts that he knows how to kill Prospero. He even tells Stefano that he can bring him to where Prospero is sleeping. He proposes that they kill Prospero, take his daughter, and set Stefano up as king of the island. Stefano thinks this a good plan, and the three prepare to set off to find Prospero. They are distracted, however, by the sound of music that Ariel plays on his flute and tabor-drum, and they decide to follow this music before executing their plot.

Alonso, Gonzalo, Sebastian, and Antonio grow weary from traveling and pause to rest. Antonio and Sebastian secretly plot to take advantage of Alonso and Gonzalo's exhaustion, deciding to kill them in the evening. Prospero, probably on the balcony of the stage and invisible to the men, causes a banquet to be set out by strangely shaped spirits. As the men prepare to eat, Ariel appears like a harpy and causes the banquet to vanish. He then accuses the men of supplanting Prospero and says that it was for this sin that Alonso's son, Ferdinand, has been taken. He vanishes, leaving Alonso feeling vexed and guilty.

Prospero now softens toward Ferdinand and welcomes him into his family as the soon-to-be-husband of Miranda. He sternly reminds Ferdinand, however, that Miranda's "virgin-knot" (IV.i.15) is not to be broken until the wedding has been officially solemnized. Prospero then asks Ariel to call forth some spirits to perform a masque for Ferdinand and Miranda. The spirits assume the shapes of Ceres, Juno, and Iris and perform a short masque celebrating the rites of marriage and the bounty of the earth. A dance of reapers and nymphs follows but is interrupted when Prospero suddenly remembers that he still must stop the plot against his life.

He sends the spirits away and asks Ariel about Trinculo, Stefano, and Caliban. Ariel tells his master of the three men's drunken plans. He also tells how he led the men with his music through prickly grass and briars and finally into a filthy pond near Prospero's cell. Ariel and Prospero then set a trap by hanging beautiful clothing in Prospero's cell. Stefano, Trinculo, and Caliban enter looking for Prospero and, finding the beautiful clothing, decide to steal it. They are immediately set upon by a pack of spirits in the shape of dogs and hounds, driven on by Prospero and Ariel.

Prospero uses Ariel to bring Alonso and the others before him. He then sends Ariel to bring the Boatswain and the mariners from where they sleep on the wrecked ship. Prospero confronts Alonso, Antonio, and Sebastian with their treachery, but tells them that he forgives them. Alonso tells him of having lost Ferdinand in the tempest and Prospero says that he recently lost his own daughter. Clarifying his meaning, he draws aside a curtain to reveal Ferdinand and Miranda playing chess. Alonso and his companions are amazed by the miracle of Ferdinand's survival, and Miranda is stunned by the sight of people unlike any she has seen before. Ferdinand tells his father about his marriage.

Ariel returns with the Boatswain and mariners. The Boatswain tells a story of having been awakened from a sleep that had apparently lasted since the tempest. At Prospero's bidding, Ariel releases Caliban, Trinculo and Stefano, who then enter wearing their stolen clothing. Prospero and Alonso command them to return it and to clean up Prospero's cell. Prospero invites Alonso and the others to stay for the night so that he can tell them the tale of his life in the past twelve years. After this, the group plans to return to Italy. Prospero, restored to his dukedom, will retire to Milan. Prospero gives Ariel one final task—to make sure the seas are calm for the return voyage-before setting him free. Finally, Prospero delivers an epilogue to the audience, asking them to forgive him for his wrongdoing and set him free by applauding.

Character List

Prospero   The play's protagonist, and father of Miranda. Twelve years before the events of the play, Prospero was the duke of Milan. His brother, Antonio, in concert with Alonso, king of Naples, usurped him, forcing him to flee in a boat with his daughter. The honest lord Gonzalo aided Prospero in his escape. Prospero has spent his twelve years on the island refining the magic that gives him the power he needs to punish and forgive his enemies.

Miranda   The daughter of Prospero, Miranda was brought to the island at an early age and has never seen any men other than her father and Caliban, though she dimly remembers being cared for by female servants as an infant. Because she has been sealed off from the world for so long, Miranda's perceptions of other people tend to be naïve and non-judgmental. She is compassionate, generous, and loyal to her father.

Ariel   Prospero's spirit helper. Ariel is referred to throughout this SparkNote and in most criticism as "he," but his gender and physical form are ambiguous. Rescued by Prospero from a long imprisonment at the hands of the witch Sycorax, Ariel is Prospero's servant until Prospero decides to release him. He is mischievous and ubiquitous, able to traverse the length of the island in an instant and to change shapes at will. He carries out virtually every task that Prospero needs accomplished in the play.

Caliban   Another of Prospero's servants. Caliban, the son of the now-deceased witch Sycorax, acquainted Prospero with the island when Prospero arrived. Caliban believes that the island rightfully belongs to him and has been stolen by Prospero. His speech and behavior is sometimes coarse and brutal, as in his drunken scenes with Stefano and Trinculo (III.ii, IV.i), and sometimes eloquent and sensitive, as in his rebukes of Prospero in Act I, scene ii, and in his description of the eerie beauty of the island in Act III, scene ii (III.ii.130-138).

Ferdinand Son and heir of Alonso. Ferdinand seems in some ways to be as pure and naïve as Miranda. He falls in love with her upon first sight and happily submits to servitude in order to win her father's approval.

Alonso King of Naples and father of Ferdinand. Alonso aided Antonio in unseating Prospero as Duke of Milan twelve years before. As he appears in the play, however, he is acutely aware of the consequences of all his actions. He blames his decision to marry his daughter to the Prince of Tunis on the apparent death of his son. In addition, after the magical banquet, he regrets his role in the usurping of Prospero.

Antonio Prospero's brother. Antonio quickly demonstrates that he is power-hungry and foolish. In Act II, scene i, he persuades Sebastian to kill the sleeping Alonso. He then goes along with Sebastian's absurd story about fending off lions when Gonzalo wakes up and catches Antonio and Sebastian with their swords drawn.

Sebastian Alonso's brother. Like Antonio, he is both aggressive and cowardly. He is easily persuaded to kill his brother in Act II, scene i, and he initiates the ridiculous story about lions when Gonzalo catches him with his sword drawn.

Gonzalo An old, honest lord, Gonzalo helped Prospero and Miranda to escape after Antonio usurped Prospero's title. Gonzalo's speeches provide an important commentary on the events of the play, as he remarks on the beauty of the island when the stranded party first lands, then on the desperation of Alonso after the magic banquet, and on the miracle of the reconciliation in Act V, scene i.

Trinculo & Stefano Trinculo, a jester, and Stefano, a drunken butler, are two minor members of the shipwrecked party. They provide a comic foil to the other, more powerful pairs of Prospero and Alonso and Antonio and Sebastian. Their drunken boasting and petty greed reflect and deflate the quarrels and power struggles of Prospero and the other noblemen.

Boatswain Appearing only in the first and last scenes, the Boatswain is vigorously good-natured. He seems competent and almost cheerful in the shipwreck scene, demanding practical help rather than weeping and prayer. And he seems surprised but not stunned when he awakens from a long sleep at the end of the play.

ANALYSIS OF MAJOR CHARACTERS

PROSPERO

Prospero is one of Shakespeare's more enigmatic protagonists. He is a sympathetic character in that he was wronged by his usurping brother, but his absolute power over the other characters and his overwrought speeches make him difficult to like. In our first glimpse of him, he appears puffed up and self-important, and his repeated insistence that Miranda pay attention suggest that his story is boring her. Once Prospero moves on to a subject other than his absorption in the pursuit of knowledge, Miranda's attention is riveted.

The pursuit of knowledge gets Prospero into trouble in the first place. By neglecting everyday matters when he was duke, he gave his brother a chance to rise up against him. His possession and use of magical knowledge renders him extremely powerful and not entirely sympathetic. His punishments of Caliban are petty and vindictive, as he calls upon his spirits to pinch Caliban when he curses. He is defensively autocratic with Ariel. For example, when Ariel reminds his master of his promise to relieve him of his duties early if he performs them willingly, Prospero bursts into fury and threatens to return him to his former imprisonment and torment. He is similarly unpleasant in his treatment of Ferdinand, leading him to his daughter and then imprisoning and enslaving him.

Despite his shortcomings as a man, however, Prospero is central to *The Tempest*'s narrative. Prospero generates the plot of the play almost single-handedly, as his various schemes, spells, and manipulations all work as part of his grand design to achieve the play's happy ending. Watching Prospero work through *The Tempest* is like watching a dramatist create a play, building a story from material at hand and developing his plot so that the resolution brings the world into line with his idea of goodness and justice. Many critics and readers of the play have interpreted Prospero as a surrogate for Shakespeare, enabling the audience to explore firsthand the ambiguities and ultimate wonder of the creative endeavor.

Prospero's final speech, in which he likens himself to a playwright by asking the audience for applause, strengthens this reading of the play, and makes the play's final scene function as a moving celebration of creativity, humanity, and art. Prospero emerges as a more likable and sympathetic figure in the final two acts of the play. In these acts, his love for Miranda, his forgiveness of his enemies, and the legitimately happy ending his scheme creates all work to mitigate some of the undesirable means he has used to achieve his happy ending. If Prospero sometimes seems autocratic, he ultimately manages to persuade the audience to share his understanding of the world—an achievement that is, after all, the final goal of every author and every play.

MIRANDA

Just under fifteen years old, Miranda is a gentle and compassionate, but also relatively passive, heroine. From her very first lines she displays a meek and emotional nature. "O, I have suffered / With those that I saw suffer!" she says of the shipwreck (I.ii.5–6), and hearing Prospero's tale of their narrow escape from Milan, she says "I, not rememb'ring how I cried out then, / Will cry it o'er again" (I.ii.133–134). Miranda does not choose her own husband. Instead, while she sleeps, Prospero sends Ariel to fetch Ferdinand, and arranges things so that the two will come to love one another. After Prospero has given the lovers his blessing, he and Ferdinand talk with surprising frankness about her virginity and the pleasures of the marriage bed while she stands quietly by. Prospero tells Ferdinand to be sure not to "break her virgin-knot" before the wedding night (IV.i.15), and Ferdinand replies with no small anticipation that lust shall never take away "the edge of that day's celebration" (IV.i.29). In the play's final scene, Miranda is presented, with Ferdinand, almost as a prop or piece of the scenery as Prospero draws aside a curtain to reveal the pair playing chess.

But while Miranda is passive in many ways, she has at least two moments of surprising forthrightness and strength that complicate the reader's impressions of her as a naïve young girl. The first such moment is in Act I, scene ii, in which she and Prospero converse with Caliban. Prospero alludes to the fact that Caliban once tried to rape Miranda. When Caliban rudely agrees that he intended to violate her, Miranda responds with impressive vehemence, clearly appalled at Caliban's light attitude toward his attempted rape. She goes on to scold him for being ungrateful for her attempts to educate him: "When thou didst not, savage, / Know thine own meaning, but wouldst gabble like / A thing most brutish, I endowed thy purposes / With words that made them known" (358–361). These lines are so surprising coming from the mouth of Miranda that many editors have amended the text and given it to Prospero. This reattribution seems to give Miranda too little credit. In Act III, scene i comes the second surprising moment—Miranda's marriage proposal to Ferdinand: "I am your wife, if you will marry me; / If not, I'll die your maid" (III.i.83–84). Her proposal comes shortly after Miranda has told herself to remember her "father's precepts" (III.i.58) forbidding conversation with Ferdinand. As the reader can see in her speech to Caliban in Act I, scene ii, Miranda is willing to speak up for herself about her sexuality.

CALIBAN

Prospero's dark, earthy slave, frequently referred to as a monster by the other characters, Caliban is the son of a witch-hag and the only real native of the island to appear in the play. He is an extremely complex figure, and he mirrors or parodies several other characters in the play. In his first speech to Prospero, Caliban insists that Prospero stole the island from him. Through this speech, Caliban suggests that his situation is much the same as Prospero's, whose brother usurped his dukedom. On the other hand, Caliban's desire for sovereignty of the island mirrors the lust for power that led Antonio to overthrow Prospero. Caliban's conspiracy with Stefano and Trinculo to murder Prospero mirrors Antonio and Sebastian's plot against Alonso, as well as Antonio and Alonso's original conspiracy against Prospero.

Caliban both mirrors and contrasts with Prospero's other servant, Ariel. While Ariel is "an airy spirit," Caliban is of the earth, his speeches turning to "springs, brine pits" (I.ii.341), "bogs, fens, flats" (II.ii.2), or crabapples and pignuts (II.ii.159–160). While Ariel maintains his dignity and his freedom by serving Prospero willingly, Caliban achieves a different kind of dignity by refusing, if only sporadically, to bow before Prospero's intimidation.

Surprisingly, Caliban also mirrors and contrasts with Ferdinand in certain ways. In Act II, scene ii Caliban enters "with a burden of wood," and Ferdinand enters in Act III, scene i "bearing a log." Both Caliban and Ferdinand profess an interest in untying

Miranda's "virgin knot." Ferdinand plans to marry her, while Caliban has attempted to rape her. The glorified, romantic, almost ethereal love of Ferdinand for Miranda starkly contrasts with Caliban's desire to impregnate Miranda and people the island with Calibans.

Finally, and most tragically, Caliban becomes a parody of himself. In his first speech to Prospero, he regretfully reminds the magician of how he showed him all the ins and outs of the island when Prospero first arrived. Only a few scenes later, however, we see Caliban drunk and fawning before a new magical being in his life: Stefano and his bottle of liquor. Soon, Caliban begs to show Stefano the island and even asks to lick his shoe. Caliban repeats the mistakes he claims to curse. In his final act of rebellion, he is once more entirely subdued by Prospero in the most petty way—he is dunked in a stinking bog and ordered to clean up Prospero's cell in preparation for dinner.

Despite his savage demeanor and grotesque appearance, however, Caliban has a nobler, more sensitive side that the audience is only allowed to glimpse briefly, and which Prospero and Miranda do not acknowledge at all. His beautiful speeches about his island home provide some of the most affecting imagery in the play, reminding the audience that Caliban really did occupy the island before Prospero came, and that he may be right in thinking his enslavement to be monstrously unjust. Caliban's swarthy appearance, his forced servitude, and his native status on the island have led many readers to interpret him as a symbol of the native cultures occupied and suppressed by European colonial societies, which are represented by the power of Prospero. Whether or not one accepts this allegory, Caliban remains one of the most intriguing and ambiguous minor characters in all of Shakespeare, a sensitive monster who allows himself to be transformed into a fool.

CHARACTER ANALYSIS

THEMES, MOTIFS & SYMBOLS

THEMES

Themes are the fundamental and often universal ideas explored in a literary work.

THE ILLUSION OF JUSTICE

The Tempest tells a fairly straightforward story involving an unjust act, the usurpation of Prospero's throne by his brother, and Prospero's quest to re-establish justice by restoring himself to power. However, the idea of justice that the play works toward seems highly subjective, since this idea represents the view of one character who controls the fate of all the other characters. Though Prospero presents himself as a victim of injustice working to right the wrongs that have been done to him, Prospero's idea of justice and injustice is somewhat hypocritical—though he is furious with his brother for taking his power, he has no qualms about enslaving Ariel and Caliban in order to achieve his ends. At many moments throughout the play, Prospero's sense of justice seems extremely one-sided and mainly involves what is good for Prospero. Moreover, because the play offers no notion of higher order or justice to supersede Prospero's interpretation of events, the play is morally ambiguous.

As the play progresses, however, it becomes more and more involved with the idea of creativity and art, and Prospero's role begins to mirror more explicitly the role of an author creating a story around him. With this metaphor in mind, and especially if we accept Prospero as a surrogate for Shakespeare himself, Prospero's sense of justice begins to seem, if not perfect, at least sympathetic. Moreover, the means he uses to achieve his idea of justice mirror the machinations of the artist, who also seeks to enable others to see his view of the world. Playwrights arrange their stories in such a way that their own idea of justice is imposed upon events. In *The Tempest,* the author is *in* the play, and the fact that he establishes his idea of justice and creates a happy ending for all the characters becomes a cause for celebration, not criticism.

By using magic and tricks that echo the special effects and spectacles of the theater, Prospero gradually persuades the other characters and the audience of the rightness of his case. As he does so, the ambiguities surrounding his methods slowly resolve themselves. Prospero forgives his enemies, releases his slaves, and relinquishes his magic power, so that, at the end of the play, he is only an old man whose work has been responsible for all the audience's pleasure. The establishment of Prospero's idea of justice becomes less a commentary on justice in life than on the nature of morality in art. Happy endings are possible, Shakespeare seems to say, because the creativity of artists can create them, even if the moral values that establish the happy ending originate from nowhere but the imagination of the artist.

THE DIFFICULTY OF DISTINGUISHING
"MEN" FROM "MONSTERS"

Upon seeing Ferdinand for the first time, Miranda says that he is "the third man that e'er I saw" (I.ii.449). The other two are, presumably, Prospero and Caliban. In their first conversation with Caliban, however, Miranda and Prospero say very little that shows they consider him to be human. Miranda reminds Caliban that before she taught him language, he gabbled "like / A thing most brutish" (I.ii.59–60) and Prospero says that he gave Caliban "human care" (I.ii.349), implying that this was something Caliban ultimately did not deserve. Caliban's exact nature continues to be slightly ambiguous later. In Act IV, scene i, reminded of Caliban's plot, Prospero refers to him as a "devil, a born devil, on whose nature / Nurture can never stick" (IV.i.188–189). Miranda and Prospero both have contradictory views of Caliban's humanity. On the one hand, they think that their education of him has lifted him from his formerly brutish status. On the other hand, they seem to see him as inherently brutish. His devilish nature can never be overcome by nurture, according to Prospero. Miranda expresses a similar sentiment in Act I, scene ii: "thy vile race, / Though thou didst learn, had that in't which good natures / Could not abide to be with" (I.ii.361–363). The inhuman part of Caliban drives out the human part, the "good nature," that is imposed on him.

Caliban claims that he was kind to Prospero, and that Prospero repaid that kindness by imprisoning him (see I.ii.347). In contrast, Prospero claims that he stopped being kind to Caliban once Caliban had tried to rape Miranda (I.ii.347–351). Which character the audience decides to believe depends on whether it views Caliban as inherently brutish, or as made brutish by oppression. The play leaves the matter ambiguous. Caliban balances all of his eloquent speeches, such as his curses in Act I, scene ii and his speech about the isle's "noises" in Act III, scene ii, with the most degrading kind of drunken, servile behavior. But Trinculo's speech upon first seeing Caliban (II.ii.18–38), the longest speech in the play, reproaches too harsh a view of Caliban and blurs the distinction between men and monsters. In England, which he visited once, Trinculo says, Caliban could be shown off for money: "There would this monster make a man. Any strange beast there makes a man. When they will not give a doit to relieve a lame beggar, they will lay out ten to see a dead Indian" (II.ii.28–31). What seems most monstrous in these sentences is not the "dead Indian," or "any strange beast," but the cruel voyeurism of those who capture and gape at them.

THE ALLURE OF RULING A COLONY

The nearly uninhabited island presents the sense of infinite possibility to almost everyone who lands there. Prospero has found it, in its isolation, an ideal place to school his daughter. Sycorax, Caliban's mother, worked her magic there after she was exiled from Algeria. Caliban, once alone on the island, now Prospero's slave, laments that he had been his own king (I.ii.344–345). As he attempts to comfort Alonso, Gonzalo imagines a utopian society on the island, over which he would rule (II.i.148–156). In Act III, scene ii, Caliban suggests that Stefano kill Prospero, and Stefano immediately envisions his own reign: "Monster, I will kill this man. His daughter and I will be King and Queen—save our graces!—and Trinculo and thyself shall be my viceroys" (III.ii.101–103). Stefano particularly looks forward to taking advantage of the spirits that make "noises" on the isle; they will provide music for his kingdom for free. All these characters envision the island as a space of freedom and unrealized potential.

The tone of the play, however, toward the hopes of the would-be colonizers is vexed at best. Gonzalo's utopian vision in Act II, scene i is undercut by a sharp retort from the usually foolish Sebastian and Antonio. When Gonzalo says that there would be no commerce or work or "sovereignty" in his society, Sebastian replies, "yet he would be king on't," and Antonio adds, "The latter end of his commonwealth forgets the beginning" (II.i.156–157). Gonzalo's fantasy thus involves him ruling the island while seeming not to rule it, and in this he becomes a kind of parody of Prospero.

While there are many representatives of the colonial impulse in the play, the colonized have only one representative: Caliban. We might develop sympathy for him at first, when Prospero seeks him out merely to abuse him, and when we see him tormented by spirits. However, this sympathy is made more difficult by his willingness to abase himself before Stefano in Act II, scene ii. Even as Caliban plots to kill one colonial master (Prospero) in Act III, scene ii, he sets up another (Stefano). The urge to rule and the urge to be ruled seem inextricably intertwined.

MOTIFS

Motifs are recurring structures, contrasts, or literary devices that can help to develop and inform the text's major themes.

MASTERS AND SERVANTS

Nearly every scene in the play either explicitly or implicitly portrays a relationship between a figure that possesses power and a figure that is subject to that power. The play explores the master-servant dynamic most harshly in cases in which the harmony of the relationship is threatened or disrupted, as by the rebellion of a servant or the ineptitude of a master. For instance, in the opening scene, the "servant" (the Boatswain) is dismissive and angry toward his "masters" (the noblemen), whose ineptitude threatens to lead to a shipwreck in the storm. From then on, master-servant relationships like these dominate the play: Prospero and Caliban; Prospero and Ariel; Alonso and his nobles; the nobles and Gonzalo; Stefano, Trinculo, and Caliban; and so forth. The play explores the psychological and social dynamics of power relationships from a number of contrasting angles, such as the generally positive relationship between Prospero and Ariel, the generally negative relationship between Prospero and Caliban, and the treachery in Alonso's relationship to his nobles.

WATER AND DROWNING

The play is awash with references to water. The Mariners enter "wet" in Act I, scene i, and Caliban, Stefano, and Trinculo enter "all wet," after being led by Ariel into a swampy lake (IV.i.193). Miranda's fear for the lives of the sailors in the "wild waters" (I.ii.2) causes her to weep. Alonso, believing his son dead because of his own actions against Prospero, decides in Act III, scene iii to drown himself. His language is echoed by Prospero in Act V, scene i when the magician promises that, once he has reconciled with his enemies, "deeper than did ever plummet sound / I'll drown my book" (V.i.56–57).

These are only a few of the references to water in the play. Occasionally, the references to water are used to compare characters. For example, the echo of Alonso's desire to drown himself in Prospero's promise to drown his book calls attention to the similarity of the sacrifices each man must make. Alonso must be willing to give up his life in order to become truly penitent and to be forgiven for his treachery against Prospero. Similarly, in order to rejoin the world he has been driven from, Prospero must be willing to give up his magic and his power.

Perhaps the most important overall effect of this water motif is to heighten the symbolic importance of the tempest itself. It is as though the water from that storm runs through the language and action of the entire play—just as the tempest itself literally and crucially affects the lives and actions of all the characters.

Mysterious Noises

The isle is indeed, as Caliban says, "full of noises" (III.ii.130). The play begins with a "tempestuous noise of thunder and lightning" (I.i.1, stage direction), and the splitting of the ship is signaled in part by "a confused noise within" (I.i.54, stage direction). Much of the noise of the play is musical, and much of the music is Ariel's. Ferdinand is led to Miranda by Ariel's music. Ariel's music also wakes Gonzalo just as Antonio and Sebastian are about to kill Alonso in Act II, scene i. Moreover, the magical banquet of Act III, scene iii is laid out to the tune of "Solemn and strange music" (III.iii.18, stage direction), and Juno and Ceres sing in the wedding masque (IV.i.106–117).

The noises, sounds, and music of the play are made most significant by Caliban's speech about the noises of the island at III.ii.130–138. Shakespeare shows Caliban in the thrall of magic, which the theater audience also experiences as the illusion of thunder, rain, invisibility. The action of *The Tempest* is very simple. What gives the play most of its hypnotic, magical atmosphere is the series of dreamlike events it stages, such as the tempest, the magical banquet, and the wedding masque. Accompanied by music, these present a feast for the eye and the ear and convince us of the magical glory of Prospero's enchanted isle.

Symbols

Symbols are objects, characters, figures, or colors used to represent abstract ideas or concepts.

The Tempest

The tempest that begins the play, and which puts all of Prospero's enemies at his disposal, symbolizes the suffering Prospero endured, and which he wants to inflict on others. All of those shipwrecked are put at the mercy of the sea, just as Prospero and his infant daughter were twelve years ago, when some loyal friends helped them out to sea in a ragged little boat (see I.ii.144–151). Prospero must make his enemies suffer as he has suffered so that they will learn from their suffering, as he has from his. The tempest is also a symbol of Prospero's magic, and of the frightening, potentially malevolent side of his power.

The Game of Chess

The object of chess is to capture the king. That, at the simplest level, is the symbolic significance of Prospero revealing Ferdinand and Miranda playing chess in the final scene. Prospero has caught the king—Alonso—and reprimanded him for his treachery. In doing so, Prospero has married Alonso's son to his own daughter without the king's knowledge, a deft political maneuver that assures Alonso's support because Alonso will have no interest in upsetting a dukedom to which his own son is heir. This is the final move in Prospero's plot, which began with the tempest. He has maneuvered the different passengers of Alonso's ship around the island with the skill of a great chess player.

Caught up in their game, Miranda and Ferdinand also symbolize something ominous about Prospero's power. They do not even notice the others staring at them for a few lines. "Sweet lord, you play me false," Miranda says, and Ferdinand assures her that he "would not for the world" do so (V.i.174–176). The theatrical tableau is almost too perfect: Ferdinand and Miranda, suddenly and unexpectedly revealed behind a curtain, playing chess and talking gently of love and faith, seem entirely removed from the world around them. Though he has promised to relinquish his magic, Prospero still seems to see his daughter as a mere pawn in his game.

PROSPERO'S BOOKS

Like the tempest, Prospero's books are a symbol of his power. "Remember / First to possess his books," Caliban says to Stefano and Trinculo, "for without them / He's but a sot" (III.ii.86–88). The books are also, however, a symbol of Prospero's dangerous desire to withdraw entirely from the world. It was his devotion to study that put him at the mercy of his ambitious brother, and it is this same devotion to study that has made him content to raise Miranda in isolation. Yet, Miranda's isolation has made her ignorant of where she came from (see I.ii.33–36), and Prospero's own isolation provides him with little company. In order to return to the world where his knowledge means something more than power, Prospero must let go of his magic.

SUMMARY & ANALYSIS

ACT I, SCENE I

SUMMARY

A violent storm rages around a small ship at sea. The master of the ship calls for his boatswain to rouse the mariners to action and prevent the ship from being run aground by the tempest. Chaos ensues. Some mariners enter, followed by a group of nobles comprised of Alonso, King of Naples, Sebastian, his brother, Antonio, Gonzalo, and others. We do not learn these men's names in this scene, nor do we learn (as we finally do in Act II, scene i) that they have just come from Tunis, in Africa, where Alonso's daughter, Claribel, has been married to the prince. As the Boatswain and his crew take in the top-sail and the topmast, Alonso and his party are merely underfoot, and the Boatswain tells them to get below-decks. Gonzalo reminds the Boatswain that one of the passengers is of some importance, but the Boatswain is unmoved. He will do what he has to in order to save the ship, regardless of who is aboard.

The lords go belowdecks, and then, adding to the chaos of the scene, three of them—Sebastian, Antonio, and Gonzalo—enter again only four lines later. Sebastian and Antonio curse the Boatswain in his labors, masking their fear with profanity. Some mariners enter wet and crying, and only at this point does the audience learn the identity of the passengers on-board. Gonzalo orders the mariners to pray for the king and the prince. There is a strange noise—perhaps the sound of thunder, splitting wood, or roaring water—and the cry of mariners. Antonio, Sebastian, and Gonzalo, preparing to sink to a watery grave, go in search of the king.

ANALYSIS

Even for a Shakespeare play, The Tempest is remarkable for its extraordinary breadth of imaginative vision. The play is steeped in magic and illusion. As a result, the play contains a tremendous amount of spectacle, yet things are often not as they seem. This opening scene certainly contains spectacle, in the form of the howling storm (the "tempest" of the play's title) tossing the little ship about and threatening to kill the characters before the play has even begun. In terms of stagecraft, it was a significant gamble for Shakespeare to open his play with this spectacular natural event, given that, in the early seventeenth century when the play was written, special effects were largely left to the audience's imagination.

Shakespeare's stage would have been almost entirely bare, without many physical signs that the actors were supposed to be on a ship, much less a ship in the midst of a lashing storm. As a result, the audience sees Shakespeare calling on all the resources of his theater to establish a certain level of realism. For example, the play begins with a "noise of thunder and lightning" (stage direction). The first word, "Boatswain!" immediately indicates that the scene is the deck of a ship. In addition, characters rush frantically in and out, often with no purpose—as when Sebastian, Antonio, and Gonzalo exit at line 29 and re-enter at 33, indicating the general level of chaos and confusion. Cries from off-stage create the illusion of a space below-decks.

But in addition to this spectacle, the play also uses its first scene to hint at some of the illusions and deceptions it will contain. Most plays of this era, by Shakespeare and others, use the introductory scene to present the main characters and hint at the general narrative to come—so Othello begins with Iago's jealousy, and King Lear begins with Lear's decision to abdicate his throne. But The Tempest begins toward the end of the actual story, late in Prospero's exile. Its opening scene is devoted to what appears to be an unexplained natural phenomenon, in which characters who are never named rush about frantically in service of no apparent plot. In fact, the confusion of the opening is itself misleading, for as we will learn later, the storm is not a natural phenomenon at all, but a deliberate magical conjuring by Prospero, designed to bring the ship to the island. The tempest is, in fact, central to the plot.

But there is more going on in this scene than initially meets the eye. The apparently chaotic exchanges of the characters introduce the important motif of master-servant relationships. The characters on the boat are divided into nobles, such as Antonio and Gonzalo, and servants or professionals, such as the Boatswain. The mortal danger of the storm upsets the usual balance between these two groups, and the Boatswain, attempting to save the ship, comes into direct conflict with the hapless nobles, who, despite their helplessness, are extremely irritated at being rudely spoken to by a commoner. The characters in the scene are never named outright; they are only referred to in terms that indicate their social stations: "Boatswain," "Master," "King," and "Prince." As the scene progresses, the characters speak less about the storm than about the class conflict underlying their attempts to survive it—a conflict between masters and servants that, as the story progresses, becomes perhaps the major motif of the play.

Gonzalo, for instance, jokes that the ship is safe because the uppity Boatswain was surely born to be hanged, not drowned in a storm: "I have great comfort from this fellow: methinks he hath no drowning mark upon him; his complexion is perfect gallows" (I.i.25–27). For his part, the Boatswain observes that social hierarchies are flimsy and unimportant in the face of nature's wrath. "What cares these roarers," he asks, referring to the booming thunder, "for the name of king?" (I.i.15–16). The irony here, of course, is that, unbeknownst to the occupants of the ship, and to the audience, the storm is not natural at all, but is in fact a product of another kind power: Prospero's magic.

ACT I, SCENE II

Due to its length, Act I, scene ii is treated in two sections.

Beginning through Miranda's awakening (I.ii.1–308)

SUMMARY

Prospero and Miranda stand on the shore of the island, having just witnessed the shipwreck. Miranda entreats her father to see that no one on-board comes to any harm. Prospero assures her that no one was harmed and tells her that it's time she learned who she is and where she comes from. Miranda seems curious, noting that Prospero has often started to tell her about herself but always stopped. However, once Prospero begins telling his tale, he asks her three times if she is listening to him. He tells her that he was once Duke of Milan and famous for his great intelligence.

Prospero explains that he gradually grew uninterested in politics, however, and turned his attention more and more to his studies, neglecting his duties as duke. This gave his brother Antonio an opportunity to act on his ambition. Working in concert with the King of Naples, Antonio usurped Prospero of his dukedom. Antonio arranged for the King of Naples to pay him an annual tribute and do him homage as duke. Later, the King of Naples helped Antonio raise an army to march on Milan, driving Prospero out. Prospero tells how he and Miranda escaped from death at the hands of the army in a barely-seaworthy boat prepared for them by his loyal subjects. Gonzalo, an honest Neapolitan, provided them with food and clothing, as well as books from Prospero's library.

Having brought Miranda up to date on how she arrived at their current home, Prospero explains that sheer good luck has brought his former enemies to the island. Miranda suddenly grows very sleepy, perhaps because Prospero charms her with his magic. When she is asleep, Prospero calls forth his spirit, Ariel. In his conversation with Ariel, we learn that Prospero and the spirit were responsible for the storm of Act I, scene i. Flying about the ship, Ariel acted as the wind, the thunder, and the lightning. When everyone except the crew had abandoned the ship, Ariel made sure, as Prospero had requested, that all were brought safely to shore but dispersed around the island. Ariel reports that the king's son is alone. He also tells Prospero that the mariners and Boatswain have been charmed to sleep in the ship, which has been brought safely to harbor. The rest of the fleet that was with the ship, believing it to have been destroyed by the storm, has headed safely back to Naples.

Prospero thanks Ariel for his service, and Ariel takes this moment to remind Prospero of his promise to take one year off of his agreed time of servitude if Ariel performs his services without complaint. Prospero does not take well to being reminded of his promises, and he chastises Ariel for his impudence. He reminds Ariel of where he came from and how Prospero rescued him. Ariel had been a servant of Sycorax, a witch banished from Algiers (Algeria) and sent to the island long ago. Ariel was too delicate a spirit to perform her horrible commands, so she imprisoned him in a "cloven pine" (I.ii.279). She did not free him before she died, and he might have remained imprisoned forever had not Prospero arrived and rescued him. Reminding Ariel of this, Prospero threatens to imprison him for twelve years if does not stop complaining. Ariel promises to be more polite. Prospero then gives him a new command: he must go make himself like a nymph of the sea and be invisible to all but Prospero. Ariel goes to do so, and Prospero, turning to Miranda's sleeping form, calls upon his daughter to awaken. She opens her eyes and, not realizing that she has been enchanted, says that the "strangeness" of Prospero's story caused her to fall asleep.

ANALYSIS

Act I, scene ii opens with the revelation that it was Prospero's magic, and not simply a hostile nature, that raised the storm that caused the shipwreck. From there, the scene moves into a long sequence devoted largely to telling the play's background story while introducing the major characters on the island. The first part of the scene is devoted to two long histories, both told by Prospero, one to Miranda and one to Ariel. If The Tempest is a play about power in various forms (as we observed in the previous scene, when the power of the storm disrupted the power relations between nobles and servants), then Prospero is the center of power, controlling events throughout the play through magic and manipulation. Prospero's retellings of past events to Miranda and Ariel do more than simply fill the audience in on the story so far. They also illustrate how Prospero maintains his power, exploring the old man's meticulous methods of controlling those around him through magic, charisma, and rhetoric.

Prospero's rhetoric is particularly important to observe in this section, especially in his confrontation with Ariel. Of all the characters in the play, Prospero alone seems to understand that controlling history enables one to control the present—that is, that one can control others by controlling how they understand the past. Prospero thus tells his story with a highly rhetorical emphasis on his own good deeds, the bad deeds of others toward him, and the ingratitude of those he has protected from the evils of others. For example, when he speaks to Miranda, he calls his brother "perfidious," then immediately says that he loved his brother better than anyone in the world except Miranda (I.ii.68). He repeatedly asks Miranda, "Dost thou attend me?" Through his questioning, he commands her attention almost hypnotically as he tells her his one-sided version of the story. Prospero himself does not seem blameless. While his brother did betray him, he also failed in his responsibilities as a ruler by giving up control of the government so that he could study. He contrasts his popularity as a leader—"the love my people bore me" (I.ii.141)—with his brother's "evil nature" (I.ii.).

When he speaks to Ariel, a magical creature over whom his mastery is less certain than over his doting daughter, Prospero goes to even greater lengths to justify himself. He treats Ariel as a combination of a pet, whom he can praise and blame as he chooses, and a pupil, demanding that the spirit recite answers to questions about the past that Prospero has taught him. Though Ariel must know the story well, Prospero says that he must "once in a month" recount Ariel's history with Sycorax, simply to ensure that his servant's fickle nature does not cause him to become disloyal. Every time he retells Ariel's history, we feel, he must increase both the persuasiveness of his own story and his control over Ariel. This is why he now chooses to claim that Ariel is behaving badly—so that he can justify a retelling of the history, even though Ariel is perfectly respectful. He forces Ariel to recall the misery he suffered while trapped in the pine tree ("thy groans / Did make wolves howl," I.ii.289–290). He then positions himself as the good savior who overthrew Sycorax's evil. However, he immediately follows this with a forceful display of his own magical power, threatening to trap Ariel in an oak just as the "evil" Sycorax had trapped him in a pine. In this way, Prospero exercises control both intellectually and physically. By controlling the way Ariel and Miranda think about their lives, he makes it difficult for them to imagine that challenging his authority would be a good thing to do, and by threatening Ariel (and, shortly thereafter, Caliban) with magical torture, he sets very high stakes for any such rebellion. For his part, Ariel promises to "do my spiriting gently" from now on.

ACT I, SCENE II (CONTINUED)

Miranda's awakening through end of the scene (I.ii.309–506)

SUMMARY

After Miranda is fully awake, Prospero suggests that they converse with their servant Caliban, the son of Sycorax. Caliban appears at Prospero's call and begins cursing. Prospero promises to punish him by giving him cramps at night, and Caliban responds by chiding Prospero for imprisoning him on the island that once belonged to him alone. He reminds Prospero that he showed him around when he first arrived. Prospero accuses Caliban of being ungrateful for all that he has taught and given him. He calls him a "lying slave" and reminds him of the effort he made to educate him (I.ii.347). Caliban's hereditary nature, he continues, makes him unfit to live among civilized people and earns him his isolation on the island. Caliban, though, cleverly notes that he knows how to curse only because Prospero and Miranda taught him to speak. Prospero then sends him away, telling him to fetch more firewood and threatening him with more cramps and aches if he refuses. Caliban obeys him.

Ariel, playing music and singing, enters and leads in Ferdinand. Prospero tells Miranda to look upon Ferdinand, and Miranda, who has seen no humans in her life other than Prospero and Caliban, immediately falls in love. Ferdinand is similarly smitten and reveals his identity as the prince of Naples. Prospero is pleased that they are so taken with each other but decides that the two must not fall in love too quickly, and so he accuses Ferdinand of merely pretending to be the prince of Naples. When he tells Ferdinand he is going to imprison him, Ferdinand draws his sword, but Prospero charms him so that he cannot move. Miranda attempts to persuade her father to have mercy, but he silences her harshly. This man, he tells her, is a mere Caliban compared to other men. He explains that she simply doesn't know any better because she has never seen any others. Prospero leads the charmed and helpless Ferdinand to his imprisonment. Secretly, he thanks the invisible Ariel for his help, sends him on another mysterious errand, and promises to free him soon.

ANALYSIS

> *You taught me language, and my profit on't*
> *Is I know how to curse. The red plague rid you*
> *For learning me your language! (I.ii.366–368)*
>   *(See* QUOTATIONS, *p. 50)*

The introduction of Caliban at the start of this section gives Prospero yet another chance to retell the history of one of the island's denizens, simultaneously filling the audience in on the background of Sycorax's unfortunate son and reasserting his power over the dour Caliban. Unlike Ariel and Miranda, however, Caliban attempts to use language as a weapon against Prospero just as Prospero uses it against Caliban. Caliban admits that he once tried to rape Miranda, but rather than showing contrition, he says that he wishes he would have been able to finish the deed, so that he could have "peopled . . . / This isle with Calibans" (I.ii.353–354). He insists that the island is his but that Prospero took it from him by flattering Caliban into teaching him about the island and then betraying and enslaving him. Prospero lists Caliban's shortcomings and describes his own good treatment of him, but Caliban answers with curses. We sense that there is more at stake here than a mere shouting-match. If words and histories are a source of power, then Prospero's control over Caliban rests on his ability to master him through words, and the closer Caliban comes to outdoing Prospero in their cursing-match, the closer Caliban comes to achieving his freedom. In the end, Caliban only relents because he fears Prospero's magic, which, he says, is so powerful that it would make a slave of his witch-mother's god, Setebos.

The re-entrance of Ariel creates an immediate and powerful contrast between Prospero's two servants. Where Caliban is coarse, resentful, and brutish, described as a "[h]ag-seed" (I.ii.368), a "poisonous" (I.ii.322) and "most lying slave" (I.ii.347) and as "earth" (I.ii.317), Ariel is delicate, refined, and gracious, described in the Dramatis personae as an "airy spirit." Ariel is indeed a spirit of air and fire, while Caliban is a creature of earth. Though the two are both Prospero's servants, Ariel serves the magician somewhat willingly, in return for his freeing him from the pine, while Caliban resists serving him at all costs. In a sense, upon arriving on the island, Prospero enslaved Caliban and freed Ariel, imprisoning the dark, earthy "monster" and releasing the bright, airy spirit. Readers who interpret The Tempest as an allegory about European colonial practices generally deem Prospero's treatment of Ariel, and especially of Caliban, to represent the disruptive effect of European colonization on native societies. Prospero's colonization has left Caliban, the original owner of the island, subject to enslavement and hatred on account of his dark countenance and—in the eyes of Prospero, a European—rough appearance.

Prospero's treatment of Ferdinand at the end of this scene re-emphasizes his power and his willingness to manipulate others to achieve his own ends. Though he is pleased by his daughter's obvious attraction to the powerful young man, Prospero does not want their love to get ahead of his plans. As a result, he has no qualms about enchanting Ferdinand and lying to Miranda about Ferdinand's unworthiness. This willingness to deceive even his beloved daughter draws attention to the moral and psychological ambiguities surrounding Shakespeare's depiction of Prospero's character.

Though many readers view The Tempest as an allegory about creativity, in which Prospero and his magic work as metaphors for Shakespeare and his art, others find Prospero's apparently narcissistic moral sense disturbing. Prospero seems to think that his own sense of justice and goodness is so well-honed and accurate that, if any other character disagrees with him, that character is wrong simply by virtue of the disagreement. He also seems to think that his objective in restoring his political power is so important that it justifies any means he chooses to use—hence his lying, his manipulations, his cursing, and the violence of his magic. Perhaps the most troubling part of all this is that Shakespeare gives us little reason to believe he disagrees with Prospero: for better or worse, Prospero is the hero of the play.

THE TEMPEST 🌿 31

ACT II, SCENE I

SUMMARY

While Ferdinand is falling in love with Miranda, Alonso, Sebastian, Antonio, Gonzalo, and other shipwrecked lords search for him on another part of the island. Alonso is quite despondent and unreceptive to the good-natured Gonzalo's attempts to cheer him up. Gonzalo meets resistance from Antonio and Sebastian as well. These two childishly mock Gonzalo's suggestion that the island is a good place to be and that they are all lucky to have survived. Alonso finally brings the repartee to a halt when he bursts out at Gonzalo and openly expresses regret at having married away his daughter in Tunis. Francisco, a minor lord, pipes up at this point that he saw Ferdinand swimming valiantly after the wreck, but this does not comfort Alonso. Sebastian and Antonio continue to provide little help. Sebastian tells his brother that he is indeed to blame for Ferdinand's death—if he had not married his daughter to an African (rather than a European), none of this would have happened.

Gonzalo tells the lords that they are only making the situation worse and attempts to change the subject, discussing what he might do if he were the lord of the island. Antonio and Sebastian mock his utopian vision. Ariel then enters, playing "solemn music" (II.i.182, stage direction), and gradually all but Sebastian and Antonio fall asleep. Seeing the vulnerability of his sleeping companions, Antonio tries to persuade Sebastian to kill his brother. He rationalizes this scheme by explaining that Claribel, who is now Queen of Tunis, is too far from Naples to inherit the kingdom should her father die, and as a result, Sebastian would be the heir to the throne. Sebastian begins to warm to the idea, especially after Antonio tells him that usurping Prospero's dukedom was the best move he ever made. Sebastian wonders aloud whether he will be afflicted by conscience, but Antonio dismisses this out of hand. Sebastian is at last convinced, and the two men draw their swords. Sebastian, however, seems to have second thoughts at the last moment and stops. While he and Antonio confer, Ariel enters with music, singing in Gonzalo's ear that a conspiracy is under way and that he should "Awake, awake!" (II.i.301). Gonzalo wakes and shouts "Preserve the King!" His exclamation wakes everyone else (II.i.303). Sebastian quickly concocts a story about hearing a loud noise that caused him and

Antonio to draw their swords. Gonzalo is obviously suspicious but does not challenge the lords. The group continues its search for Ferdinand.

ANALYSIS

As in the storm scene in Act I, scene i, Shakespeare emphasizes and undercuts the capacity of the bare stage to create a convincing illusion throughout Act II, scene i. As the shipwrecked mariners look around the island, they describe it in poetry of great imagistic richness, giving the audience an imaginary picture of the setting of the play. Even so, they disagree about what they see, and even argue over what the island actually looks like. Adrian finds it to be of "subtle, tender, and delicate temperance," where "the air breathes upon us . . . most sweetly" (II.i.42–47). Gonzalo says that the grass is "lush and lusty" and "green" (II.i.53–54). Antonio and Sebastian, however, cynical to the last, refuse to let these descriptions rest in the audience's mind. They say that the air smells "as 'twere perfumed by a fen" (II.i.49), meaning a swamp, and that the ground "indeed is tawny" (II.i.55), or brown. The remarks of Antonio and Sebastian could be easily discounted as mere grumpiness, were it not for the fact that Gonzalo and Adrian do seem at times to be stretching the truth. (Adrian, for example, begins his remarks about the island's beauty by saying, "Though this island seem to be desert . . . Uninhabitable, and almost inaccessible" [II.i.35–38].) Thus the bareness of the stage allows the beauty and other qualities of the island to be largely a matter of perspective. The island may be a paradise, but only if one chooses to see it that way.

Shakespeare uses this ambiguous setting for several different purposes. First, the setting heightens the sense of wonder and mystery that surrounds the magical island. It also gives each audience member a great deal of freedom to imagine the island as he or she so chooses. Most importantly, however, it enables the island to work as a reflection of character—we know a great deal about different characters simply from how they choose to see the island. Hence the dark, sensitive Caliban can find it both a place of terror—as when he enters, frightened and overworked in Act II, scene ii—and of great beauty—as in his "the isle is full of noises" speech (III.ii.130–138). Therefore, both Gonzalo (at II.i.147–164) and Trinculo (throughout Act III, scene ii), colonially minded, are so easily able to imagine it as the site of their own utopian societies.

Gonzalo's fantasy about the plantation he would like to build on the island is a remarkable poetic evocation of a utopian society, in which no one would work, all people would be equal and live off the land, and all women would be "innocent and pure." This vision indicates something of Gonzalo's own innocence and purity. Shakespeare treats the old man's idea of the island as a kind of lovely dream, in which the frustrations and obstructions of life (magistrates, wealth, power) would be removed and all could live naturally and authentically. Though Gonzalo's idea is not presented as a practical possibility (hence the mockery he receives from Sebastian and Antonio), Gonzalo's dream contrasts to his credit with the power-obsessed ideas of most of the other characters, including Prospero. Gonzalo would do away with the very master-servant motif that lies at the heart of The Tempest.

The mockery dished out by Antonio and Sebastian reveals, by contrast, something of the noblemen's cynicism and lack of feeling. Where Gonzalo is simply grateful and optimistic about having survived the shipwreck, Antonio and Sebastian seem mainly to be annoyed by it, though not so annoyed that they stop their incessant jesting with each other. Gonzalo says that they are simply loud-mouthed jokers, who "would lift the moon out of her sphere, if she would continue in it five weeks without changing" (II.i.179–181). By conspiring against the king, however, they reveal themselves as more sinister and greedier than Gonzalo recognizes, using their verbal wit to cover up their darker and more wicked impulses. However, their greediness for power is both foolish and clumsy. As they attempt to cover their treachery with the story of the "bellowing / Like bulls, or rather lions" (II.i.307–308), it seems hard to believe that Antonio ever could have risen successfully against his brother. The absurdly aggressive behavior of Antonio and Sebastian makes Prospero's exercise of power in the previous and following scenes seem necessary. It also puts Alonso in a sympathetic position. He is a potential victim of the duo's treachery, a fact that helps the audience believe his conversion when he reconciles with Prospero at the end.

ACT II, SCENE II

SUMMARY

Caliban enters with a load of wood, and thunder sounds in the background. Caliban curses and describes the torments that Prospero's spirits subject him to: they pinch, bite, and prick him, especially when he curses. As he is thinking of these spirits, Caliban sees Trinculo and imagines him to be one of the spirits. Hoping to avoid pinching, he lies down and covers himself with his cloak. Trinculo hears the thunder and looks about for some cover from the storm. The only thing he sees is the cloak-covered Caliban on the ground. He is not so much repulsed by Caliban as curious. He cannot decide whether Caliban is a "man or a fish" (II.ii.24). He thinks of a time when he traveled to England and witnessed freak-shows there. Caliban, he thinks, would bring him a lot of money in England. Thunder sounds again and Trinculo decides that the best shelter in sight is beneath Caliban's cloak, and so he joins the man-monster there.

Stefano enters singing and drinking. He hears Caliban cry out to Trinculo, "Do not torment me! O!" (II.ii.54). Hearing this and seeing the four legs sticking out from the cloak, Stefano thinks the two men are a four-legged monster with a fever. He decides to relieve this fever with a drink. Caliban continues to resist Trinculo, whom he still thinks is a spirit tormenting him. Trinculo recognizes Stefano's voice and says so. Stefano, of course, assumes for a moment that the monster has two heads, and he promises to pour liquor in both mouths. Trinculo now calls out to Stefano, and Stefano pulls his friend out from under the cloak. While the two men discuss how they arrived safely on shore, Caliban enjoys the liquor and begs to worship Stefano. The men take full advantage of Caliban's drunkenness, mocking him as a "most ridiculous monster" (II.ii.157) as he promises to lead them around and show them the isle.

ANALYSIS

Trinculo and Stefano are the last new characters to be introduced in the play. They act as comic foils to the main action, and will in later acts become specific parodies of Antonio and Sebastian. At this point, their role is to present comically some of the more serious issues in the play concerning Prospero and Caliban. In Act I, scene ii, Prospero calls Caliban a "slave" (II.ii.311, 322, 347), "thou earth" (II.ii.317), "Filth" (II.ii.349), and "Hag-seed" (II.ii.368). Stefano and Trinculo's epithet of choice in Act II, scene ii and thereafter is "monster." But while these two make quite clear that Caliban is seen as less than human by the Europeans on the island, they also treat him more humanely than Prospero does. Stefano and Trinculo, a butler and a jester respectively, remain at the low end of the social scale in the play, and have little difficulty finding friendship with the strange islander they meet. "Misery acquaints a man with strange bedfellows," says Trinculo (II.ii.36–37), and then hastens to crawl beneath Caliban's garment in order to get out of the rain. The similarity, socially and perhaps physically as well, between Trinculo and Caliban is further emphasized when Stefano, drunk, initially mistakes the two for a single monster: "This is some monster of the isle with four legs" (II.ii.62).

More important than the emphasis on the way in which Caliban seems to others more monster than man, is the way in which this scene dramatizes the initial encounter between an almost completely isolated, "primitive" culture and a foreign, "civilized" one. The reader discovers during Caliban and Prospero's confrontation in Act I, scene ii that Prospero initially "made much of" Caliban (II.ii.336); that he gave Caliban "Water with berries in't" (II.ii.337); that Caliban showed him around the island; and that Prospero later imprisoned Caliban, after he had taken all he could take from him. The reader can see these events in Act II, scene ii, with Trinculo and Stefano in the place of Prospero. Stefano calls Caliban a "brave monster," as they set off singing around the island. In addition, Stefano and Trinculo give Caliban wine, which Caliban finds to be a "celestial liquor" (II.ii.109). Moreover, Caliban initially mistakes Stefano and Trinculo for Prospero's spirits, but alcohol convinces him that Stefano is a "brave god" and decides unconditionally to "kneel to him" (II.ii.109–110). This scene shows the foreign, civilized culture as decadent and manipulative: Stefano immediately plans to "inherit" the island (II.ii.167), using Caliban to show him all its virtues. Stefano and Trinculo are a grotesque, parodic version of Prospero upon his arrival twelve years ago. Godlike in the eyes of the native, they slash and burn their way to power.

By this point, Caliban has begun to resemble a parody of himself. Whereas he would "gabble like / A thing most brutish" (I.ii.359–360) upon Prospero's arrival, because he did not know language, he now is willfully inarticulate in his drunkenness. Immediately putting aside his fear that these men are spirits sent to do him harm, Caliban puts his trust in them for all the wrong reasons. What makes Caliban's behavior in this scene so tragic is that we might expect him, especially after his eloquent curses of Prospero in Act I, scene ii, to know better.

ACT III, SCENE I

SUMMARY

> *I am your wife, if you will marry me.*
> *If not, I'll die your maid. To be your fellow*
> *You may deny me, but I'll be your servant*
> *Whether you will or no.*
>
> *(See* QUOTATIONS, *p. 52 51)*

Back at Prospero's cell, Ferdinand takes over Caliban's duties and carries wood for Prospero. Unlike Caliban, however, Ferdinand has no desire to curse. Instead, he enjoys his labors because they serve the woman he loves, Miranda. As Ferdinand works and thinks of Miranda, she enters, and after her, unseen by either lover, Prospero enters. Miranda tells Ferdinand to take a break from his work, or to let her work for him, thinking that her father is away. Ferdinand refuses to let her work for him but does rest from his work and asks Miranda her name. She tells him, and he is pleased: "Miranda" comes from the same Latin word that gives English the word "admiration." Ferdinand's speech plays on the etymology: "Admired Miranda! / Indeed the top of admiration, worth / What's dearest to the world!" (III.i.37–39).

Ferdinand goes on to flatter his beloved. Miranda is, of course, modest, pointing out that she has no idea of any woman's face but her own. She goes on to praise Ferdinand's face, but then stops herself, remembering her father's instructions that she should not speak to Ferdinand. Ferdinand assures Miranda that he is a prince and probably a king now, though he prays his father is not dead. Miranda seems unconcerned with Ferdinand's title, and asks only if he loves her. Ferdinand replies enthusiastically that he does, and his response emboldens Miranda to propose marriage. Ferdinand accepts and the two part. Prospero comes forth, subdued in his happiness, for he has known that this would happen. He then hastens to his book of magic in order to prepare for remaining business.

ANALYSIS

> *There be some sports are painful, and their labour*
> *Delight in them sets off. Some kinds of baseness*
> *Are nobly undergone, and most poor matters*
> *Point to rich ends. This my mean task*

Would be as heavy to me as odious, but
The mistress which I serve quickens what's dead
And makes my labours pleasures.

(See QUOTATIONS, *p. 51)*

This scene revolves around different images of servitude. Ferdinand is literally in service to Prospero, but in order to make his labor more pleasant he sees Miranda as his taskmaster. When he talks to Miranda, Ferdinand brings up a different kind of servitude—the love he has felt for a number of other beautiful women. Ferdinand sees this love, in comparison to his love for Miranda, as an enforced servitude: "Full many a lady / I have eyed with the best regard, and many a time / Th' harmony of their tongues hath into bondage / Brought my too diligent ear" (III.i.39–42). When Miranda stops the conversation momentarily, remembering her father's command against talking to Ferdinand, the prince hastens to assure her that he is worthy of her love. He is royalty, he says, and in normal life "would no more endure / This wooden slavery [carrying logs] than to suffer / The flesh-fly blow my mouth" (III.i.61–63). But this slavery is made tolerable by a different kind of slavery: "The very instant that I saw you did / My heart fly to your service; there resides, / To make me slave to it" (III.i.64–66). The words "slavery" and "slave" underscore the parallel as well as the difference between Ferdinand and Caliban. Prospero repeatedly calls Caliban a slave, and we see Caliban as a slave both to Prospero and to his own anger. Ferdinand, on the other hand, is a willing slave to his love, happy in a servitude that makes him rejoice rather than curse.

At the end of the scene, Miranda takes up the theme of servitude. Proposing marriage to Ferdinand, she says that "I am your wife, if you will marry me; / If not, I'll die your maid. . . . / You may deny me; but I'll be your servant / Whether you will or no" (III.i.83–86). This is the only scene of actual interaction we see between Ferdinand and Miranda. Miranda is, as we know, and as she says, very innocent: "I do not know / One of my sex, no woman's face remember / Save from my glass mine own; nor have I seen / More that I may call men than you, good friend, / And my dear father" (III.i.48–52). The play has to make an effort to overcome the implausibility of this court-ship—to make Miranda look like something more than Prospero's puppet and a fool for the first man she sees. Shakespeare accomplishes this by showing Ferdinand in one kind of servitude—in which he must literally and physically humble himself—as he talks earnestly about another kind of servitude, in which he gives himself wholly to Miranda. The fact that Miranda speaks of a similar servitude of her own accord, that she remembers her father's "precepts" and then disregards them, and that Prospero remains in the background without interfering helps the audience to trust this meeting between the lovers more than their first meeting in Act I, scene ii.

Of course, Prospero's presence in the first place may suggest that he is somehow in control of what Miranda does or says. At the end he steps forward to assure the audience that he knew what would happen: "So glad of this as they I cannot be, / Who are surprised with all" (III.i.93–94). But Prospero's five other lines (III.i.31–32 and III.i.74–76) do not suggest that he controls what Miranda says. Rather, he watches in the manner of a father—both proud of his daughter's choice and slightly sad to see her grow up.

ACT III, SCENE II

SUMMARY

Caliban, Trinculo, and Stefano continue to drink and wander about the island. Stefano now refers to Caliban as "servant monster" and repeatedly orders him to drink. Caliban seems happy to obey. The men begin to quarrel, mostly in jest, in their drunkenness. Stefano has now assumed the title of Lord of the Island and he promises to hang Trinculo if Trinculo should mock his servant monster. Ariel, invisible, enters just as Caliban is telling the men that he is "subject to a tyrant, a sorcerer, that by his cunning hath cheated me of the island" (III.ii.40–41). Ariel begins to stir up trouble, calling out, "Thou liest" (III.ii.42). Caliban cannot see Ariel and thinks that Trinculo said this. He threatens Trinculo, and Stefano tells Trinculo not to interrupt Caliban anymore. Trinculo protests that he said nothing. Drunkenly, they continue talking, and Caliban tells them of his desire to get revenge against Prospero. Ariel continues to interrupt now and then with the words, "Thou liest." Ariel's ventriloquizing ultimately results in Stefano hitting Trinculo.

While Ariel looks on, Caliban plots against Prospero. The key, Caliban tells his friends, is to take Prospero's magic books. Once they have done this, they can kill Prospero and take his daughter. Stefano will become king of the island and Miranda will be his queen. Trinculo tells Stefano that he thinks this plan is a good idea, and Stefano apologizes for the previous quarreling. Caliban assures them that Prospero will be asleep within the half hour.

Ariel plays a tune on his flute and tabor-drum. Stefano and Trinculo wonder at this noise, but Caliban tells them it is nothing to fear. Stefano relishes the thought of possessing this island kingdom "where I shall have my music for nothing" (III.ii.139–140). Then the men decide to follow the music and afterward to kill Prospero.

ANALYSIS

As we have seen, one of the ways in which The Tempest builds its rich aura of magical and mysterious implication is through the use of doubles: scenes, characters, and speeches that mirror each other by either resemblance or contrast. This scene is an example of doubling: almost everything in it echoes Act II, scene i. In this scene, Caliban, Trinculo, and Stefano wander aimlessly about the island, and Stefano muses about the kind of island it would be if he ruled it—"I will kill this man [Prospero]. His daughter and I will be King and Queen . . . and Trinculo and thyself [Caliban] shall be viceroys" (III.ii.101–103)—just as Gonzalo had done while wandering with Antonio and Sebastian in Act II, scene i. At the end of Act III, scene ii, Ariel enters, invisible, and causes strife among the group, first with his voice and then with music, leading the men astray in order to thwart Antonio and Sebastian's plot against Alonso. The power-hungry servants Stefano and Trinculo thus become rough parodies of the power-hungry courtiers Antonio and Sebastian. All four men are now essentially equated with Caliban, who is, as Alonso and Antonio once were, simply another usurper.

But Caliban also has a moment in this scene to become more than a mere usurper: his striking and apparently heartfelt speech about the sounds of the island. Reassuring the others not to worry about Ariel's piping, Caliban says:

> The isle is full of noises,
> Sounds and sweet airs, that give delight and hurt not.
> Sometimes a thousand twangling instruments
> Will hum about mine ears, and sometime voices,
> That, if I then had waked after long sleep,
> Will make me sleep again: and then, in dreaming,
> The clouds methought would open and show riches
> Ready to drop upon me, that, when I waked,
> I cried to dream again. (III.ii.130–138)

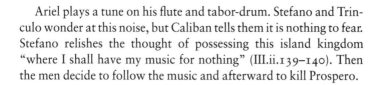

SUMMARY & ANALYSIS

In this speech, we are reminded of Caliban's very close connection to the island—a connection we have seen previously only in his speeches about showing Prospero or Stefano which streams to drink from and which berries to pick (I.ii.333–347 and II.ii.152–164). After all, Caliban is not only a symbolic "native" in the colonial allegory of the play. He is also an actual native of the island, having been born there after his mother Sycorax fled there. This ennobling monologue—ennobling because there is no servility in it, only a profound understanding of the magic of the island—provides Caliban with a moment of freedom from Prospero and even from his drunkenness. In his anger and sadness, Caliban seems for a moment to have risen above his wretched role as Stefano's fool. Throughout much of the play, Shakespeare seems to side with powerful figures such as Prospero against weaker figures such as Caliban, allowing us to think, with Prospero and Miranda, that Caliban is merely a monster. But in this scene, he takes the extraordinary step of briefly giving the monster a voice. Because of this short speech, Caliban becomes a more understandable character, and even, for the moment at least, a sympathetic one.

ACT III, SCENE III

SUMMARY

Alonso, Sebastian, Antonio, Gonzalo, and their companion lords become exhausted, and Alonso gives up all hope of finding his son. Antonio, still hoping to kill Alonso, whispers to Sebastian that Alonso's exhaustion and desperation will provide them with the perfect opportunity to kill the king later that evening.

At this point "solemn and strange music" fills the stage (III.iii.17, stage direction), and a procession of spirits in "several strange shapes" enters, bringing a banquet of food (III.iii.19, stage direction). The spirits dance about the table, invite the king and his party to eat, and then dance away. Prospero enters at this time as well, having rendered himself magically invisible to everyone but the audience. The men disagree at first about whether to eat, but Gonzalo persuades them it will be all right, noting that travelers are returning every day with stories of unbelievable but true events. This, he says, might be just such an event.

Just as the men are about to eat, however, a noise of thunder erupts, and Ariel enters in the shape of a harpy. He claps his wings upon the table and the banquet vanishes. Ariel mocks the men for attempting to draw their swords, which magically have been made to feel heavy. Calling himself an instrument of Fate and Destiny, he goes on to accuse Alonso, Sebastian, and Antonio of driving Prospero from Milan and leaving him and his child at the mercy of the sea. For this sin, he tells them, the powers of nature and the sea have exacted revenge on Alonso by taking Ferdinand. He vanishes, and the procession of spirits enters again and removes the banquet table. Prospero, still invisible, applauds the work of his spirit and announces with satisfaction that his enemies are now in his control. He leaves them in their distracted state and goes to visit with Ferdinand and his daughter.

Alonso, meanwhile, is quite desperate. He has heard the name of Prospero once more, and it has signaled the death of his own son. He runs to drown himself. Sebastian and Antonio, meanwhile, decide to pursue and fight with the spirits. Gonzalo, ever the voice of reason, tells the other, younger lords to run after Antonio, Sebastian, and Alonso and to make sure that none of the three does anything rash.

ANALYSIS

Ariel's appearance as an avenging harpy represents the climax of Prospero's revenge, as Antonio, Alonso, and the other lords are confronted with their crimes and threatened with punishment. From Prospero's perspective, the disguised Ariel represents justice and the powers of nature. He has arrived to right the wrongs that have been done to Prospero, and to punish the wicked for their sins. However, the audience knows that Ariel is not an angel or representative of a higher moral power, but merely mouths the script that Prospero has taught him. Ariel's only true concern, of course, is to win his freedom from Prospero. Thus, the vision of justice presented in this scene is artificial and staged.

Ariel's display has less to do with fate or justice than with Prospero's ability to manipulate the thoughts and feelings of others. Just as his frequent recitations of history to Ariel, Miranda, and Caliban are designed to govern their thinking by imposing his own rhetoric upon it, Prospero's decision to use Ariel as an illusory instrument of "fate" is designed to govern the thinking of the nobles at the table by imposing his own ideas of justice and right action upon their minds. Whether or not Prospero's case is really just—as it may well be—his use of Ariel in this scene is done purely to further his persuasion and control. He knows that a supernatural creature claiming to represent nature will make a greater impression in advancing his argument than he himself could hope to. If Prospero simply appeared before the table and stated his case, it would seem tainted with selfish desire. However, for Ariel to present Prospero's case in this fashion makes it seem like the inevitable natural order of the universe—even though Prospero himself is behind everything Ariel says.

This state of affairs gets at the heart of the central problem of reading The Tempest. The play seems to present Prospero's notion of justice as the only viable one, but it simultaneously undercuts Prospero's notion of justice by presenting the artificiality of his method of obtaining justice. We are left to wonder if justice really exists when it appears that only a sorcerer can bring about justice. Alternatively, Prospero's manipulations may put us in mind of what playwrights do when they arrange events into meaningful patterns, rewarding the good and punishing the bad.

ACT IV, SCENE I

SUMMARY

Prospero gives his blessing to Ferdinand and Miranda, warning Ferdinand only that he take care not to break Miranda's "virgin-knot" before the wedding has been solemnized (IV.i.15–17). Ferdinand promises to comply. Prospero then calls in Ariel and asks him to summon spirits to perform a masque for Ferdinand and Miranda. Soon, three spirits appear in the shapes of the mythological figures of Iris (Juno's messenger and the goddess of the rainbow), Juno (queen of the gods), and Ceres (goddess of agriculture). This trio performs a masque celebrating the lovers' engagement. First, Iris enters and asks Ceres to appear at Juno's wish, to celebrate "a contract of true love." Ceres appears, and then Juno enters. Juno and Ceres together bless the couple, with Juno wishing them honor and riches, and Ceres wishing them natural prosperity and plenty. The spectacle awes Ferdinand and he says that he would like to live on the island forever, with Prospero as his father and Miranda as his wife. Juno and Ceres send Iris to fetch some nymphs and reapers to perform a country dance. Just as this dance begins, however, Prospero startles suddenly and then sends the spirits away. Prospero, who had forgotten about Caliban's plot against him, suddenly remembers that the hour nearly has come for Caliban and the conspirators to make their attempt on his life.

Our revels now are ended. These our actors,
As I foretold you, were all spirits, and
Are melted into air, into thin air;
And, like the baseless fabric of this vision,
The cloud-capped towers, the gorgeous palaces,
The solemn temples, the great globe itself,
Yea, all which it inherit, shall dissolve;
And, like this insubstantial pageant faded,
Leave not a rack behind. We are such stuff
As dreams are made on, and our little life
Is rounded with a sleep. (IV.i.148–158)

Prospero's apparent anger alarms Ferdinand and Miranda, but
Prospero assures the young couple that his consternation is largely a
result of his age; he says that a walk will soothe him. Prospero makes
a short speech about the masque, saying that the world itself is as
insubstantial as a play, and that human beings are "such stuff / As
dreams are made on." Ferdinand and Miranda leave Prospero to
himself, and the old enchanter immediately summons Ariel, who
seems to have made a mistake by not reminding Prospero of Caliban's
plot before the beginning of the masque. Prospero now asks Ariel to tell
him again what the three conspirators are up to, and Ariel tells him of
the men's drunken scheme to steal Prospero's book and kill him. Ariel
reports that he used his music to lead these men through rough and
prickly briars and then into a filthy pond. Prospero thanks his trusty
spirit, and the two set a trap for the three would-be assassins.

On a clothesline in Prospero's cell, Prospero and Ariel hang an array
of fine apparel for the men to attempt to steal, after which they render
themselves invisible. Caliban, Trinculo, and Stefano enter, wet from the
filthy pond. The fine clothing immediately distracts Stefano and Trinculo. They want to steal it, despite the protests of Caliban, who wants
to stick to the plan and kill Prospero. Stefano and Trinculo ignore him.
Soon after they touch the clothing, there is "A noise of hunters"
(IV.i.251, stage direction). A pack of spirits in the shape of hounds, set
on by Ariel and Prospero, drives the thieves out.

────────────────

ANALYSIS
The wedding of Ferdinand and Miranda draws near. Thus, Act IV,
scene i explores marriage from several different angles. Prospero and
Ferdinand's surprisingly coarse discussion of Miranda's virginity at the
beginning of the scene serves to emphasize the disparity in knowledge

SUMMARY & ANALYSIS

and experience between Miranda and her future husband. Prospero has kept his daughter extremely innocent. As a result, Ferdinand's vulgar description of the pleasures of the wedding-bed reminds the audience (and probably Prospero as well) that the end of Miranda's innocence is now imminent. Her wedding-night will come, she will lose her virginity, and she will be in some way changed. This discussion is a blunt reminder that change is inevitable and that Miranda will soon give herself, in an entirely new way, to a man besides her father. Though Prospero somewhat perfunctorily initiates and participates in the sexual discussion, he also seems to be affected by it. In the later parts of the scene, he makes unprecedented comments on the transitory nature of life and on his own old age. Very likely, the prospect of Miranda's marriage and growing up calls these ideas to his mind.

After the discussion of sexuality, Prospero introduces the masque, which moves the exploration of marriage to the somewhat more comfortable realms of society and family. In the sixteenth and seventeenth centuries, masques were popular forms of entertainment in England. Masques featured masked actors performing allegorical, often highly ritualized stories drawn from mythology and folklore. Prospero's masque features Juno, the symbol of marriage and family life in Roman mythology, and Ceres, the symbol of agriculture, and thus of nature, growth, prosperity, and rebirth, all notions intimately connected to marriage. The united blessing of the union by Juno and Ceres is a blessing on the couple that wishes them prosperity and wealth while explicitly tying their marriage to notions of social propriety (Juno wishes them "honor") and harmony with the Earth. In this way, marriage is subtly glorified as both the foundation of society and as part of the natural order of things, given the accord between marriage and nature in Ceres' speech.

Interestingly, Juno and Ceres de-emphasize the role of love, personal feeling, and sexuality in marriage, choosing instead to focus on marriage's place in the social and natural orders. When Ceres wonders to Iris where Venus and Cupid, the deities of love and sex, are, she says that she hopes not to see them because their lustful powers caused Pluto, god of the underworld, to kidnap Persephone, Ceres's daughter (IV.i.86–91). Iris assures Ceres that Venus and Cupid are nowhere in sight. Venus and Cupid had hoped to foil the purity of the impending union, "but in vain" (IV.i.97). Ceres, Juno, and Iris have kept the gods of lust at bay; it seems that, through his masque, Prospero is trying to suppress entirely the lasciviousness of Ferdinand's tone when he discusses Miranda's virginity.

In almost all of Shakespeare's comedies, marriage is used as a symbol of a harmonious and healthy social order. In these plays, misunderstandings erupt, conflicts break out, and at the end, love triumphs and marriage sets everything right. The Tempest, a romance, is not exactly a comedy. However, it is deeply concerned with the social order, both in terms of the explicit conflict of the play (Prospero's struggle to regain his place as duke) and in terms of the play's constant exploration of the master-servant dynamic, especially when the dynamic appears unsettled or discordant. One reason Shakespeare might shift the focus of the play to marriage at this point is to prepare the audience for the mending of the disrupted social order that takes place at the end of the story. Calling upon all the social and dramatic associations of marriage, and underscoring them heavily with the solemnity of the masque, Shakespeare creates a sense that, even though the play's major conflict is still unresolved, the world of the play is beginning to heal itself. What is interesting about this technique is that the sense of healing has little to do with anything intrinsic to the characters themselves. Throughout this scene, Ferdinand seems unduly coarse, Miranda merely a threatened innocent, and Prospero somewhat weary and sad. But the fact of marriage itself, as it is presented in the masque, is enough to settle the turbulent waters of the story.

After this detailed exploration of marriage, the culmination of Caliban's plot against Prospero occurs merely as a moment of comic relief, exposing the weaknesses of Stefano and Trinculo and giving the conspirators their just deserts. Any hint of sympathy we may have had for Caliban earlier in the play has vanished, partly because Caliban's behavior has been vicious and degraded, but also because Prospero has become more appealing. Prospero has come to seem more fully human because of his poignant feelings for his daughter and his discussion of his old age. As a result, he is far easier to identify with than he was in the first Act. Simply by accenting aspects of character we have already seen, namely Prospero's love for Miranda and the conspirators' absurd incompetence, Shakespeare substantially rehabilitates Prospero in the eyes of the audience. We can cheer wholeheartedly for Prospero in his humorous defeat of Caliban now; this is one of the first really uncomplicated moments in the play. After this moment, Prospero becomes easier to sympathize with as the rest of the story unfolds.

ACT V, SCENE I & EPILOGUE

SUMMARY

Ariel tells Prospero that the day has reached its "sixth hour" (6 P.M.), when Ariel is allowed to stop working. Prospero acknowledges Ariel's request and asks how the king and his followers are faring. Ariel tells him that they are currently imprisoned, as Prospero ordered, in a grove. Alonso, Antonio, and Sebastian are mad with fear; and Gonzalo, Ariel says, cries constantly. Prospero tells Ariel to go release the men, and now alone on stage, delivers his famous soliloquy in which he gives up magic. He says he will perform his last task and then break his staff and drown his magic book.

Ariel now enters with Alonso and his companions, who have been charmed and obediently stand in a circle. Prospero speaks to them in their charmed state, praising Gonzalo for his loyalty and chiding the others for their treachery. He then sends Ariel to his cell to fetch the clothes he once wore as Duke of Milan. Ariel goes and returns immediately to help his master to put on the garments. Prospero promises to grant freedom to his loyal helper-spirit and sends him to fetch the Boatswain and mariners from the wrecked ship. Ariel goes.

Prospero releases Alonso and his companions from their spell and speaks with them. He forgives Antonio but demands that Antonio return his dukedom. Antonio does not respond and does not, in fact, say a word for the remainder of the play except to note that Caliban is "no doubt marketable" (V.i.269). Alonso now tells Prospero of the missing Ferdinand. Prospero tells Alonso that he, too, has lost a child in this last tempest—his daughter. Alonso continues to be wracked with grief. Prospero then draws aside a curtain, revealing behind it Ferdinand and Miranda, who are playing a game of chess. Alonso is ecstatic at the discovery. Meanwhile, the sight of more humans impresses Miranda. Alonso embraces his son and daughter-in-law to be and begs Miranda's forgiveness for the treacheries of twelve years ago. Prospero silences Alonso's apologies, insisting that the reconciliation is complete.

After arriving with the Boatswain and mariners, Ariel is sent to fetch Caliban, Trinculo, and Stefano, which he speedily does. The three drunken thieves are sent to Prospero's cell to return the clothing they stole and to clean it in preparation for the evening's reveling. Prospero then invites Alonso and his company to stay the night. He will tell them the tale of his last twelve years, and in the morning, they can all set out for Naples, where Miranda and Ferdinand will be married. After the wedding, Prospero will return to Milan, where he plans to contemplate the end of his life. The last charge Prospero gives to Ariel before setting him free is to make sure the trip home is made on "calm seas" with "auspicious gales" (V.i.318).

The other characters exit, and Prospero delivers the epilogue. He describes the loss of his magical powers ("Now my charms are all o'erthrown") and says that, as he imprisoned Ariel and Caliban, the audience has now imprisoned him on the stage. He says that the audience can only release him by applauding, and asks them to remember that his only desire was to please them. He says that, as his listeners would like to have their own crimes forgiven, they should forgive him, and set him free by clapping.

ANALYSIS

In this scene, all of the play's characters are brought on stage together for the first time. Prospero repeatedly says that he is relinquishing his magic, but its presence pervades the scene. He enters in his magic robes. He brings Alonso and the others into a charmed circle (V.i.57, stage direction) and holds them there for about fifty lines. Once he releases them from the spell, he makes the magician-like spectacle of unveiling Miranda and Ferdinand behind a curtain, playing chess (V.i.173, stage direction). His last words of the play proper are a command to Ariel to ensure for him a safe voyage home. Only in the epilogue, when he is alone on-stage, does Prospero announce definitively that his charms are "all o'erthrown" (V.i.1).

When Prospero passes judgment on his enemies in the final scene, we are no longer put off by his power, both because his love for Miranda has humanized him to a great extent, and also because we now can see that, over the course of the play, his judgments generally have been justified. Gonzalo is an "honourable man" (V.i.62); Alonso did, and knows he did, treat Prospero "[m]ost cruelly" (V.i.71); and Antonio is an "[u]nnatural" brother (V.i.79). Caliban, Stefano, and Trinculo, led in sheepishly in their stolen apparel at line 258, are so foolish as to deserve punishment, and Prospero's command that they "trim" his cell "handsomely" (V.i.297) in preparation for the evening's revels seems mild. Accusing his enemies neither more nor less than they deserve, and forgiving them instantly once he has been restored to his dukedom, Prospero has at last come to seem judicious rather than arbitrary in his use of power.

Of course, it helps that Prospero's most egregious sins have been mitigated by the outcome of events. He will no longer hold Ariel and Caliban as slaves because he is giving up his magic and returning to Naples. Moreover, he will no longer dominate Miranda because she is marrying Ferdinand.

Prospero has made the audience see the other characters clearly and accurately. What is remarkable is the fact that the most sympathetic character in the play, Miranda, still cannot. Miranda's last lines are her most famous: "O wonder!" she exclaims upon seeing the company Prospero has assembled. "How many goodly creatures are there here! / How beauteous mankind is! O brave new world / That has such people in't!" (V.i.184–187). From Miranda's innocent perspective, such a remark seems genuine and even true. But from the audience's perspective, it must seem somewhat ridiculous. After all, Antonio and Sebastian are still surly and impudent; Alonso has repented only after believing his son to be dead; and Trinculo and Stefano are drunken, petty thieves. However, Miranda speaks from the perspective of someone who has not seen any human being except her father since she was three years old. She is merely delighted by the spectacle of all these people.

In a sense, her innocence may be shared to some extent by the playwright, who takes delight in creating and presenting a vast array of humanity, from kings to traitors, from innocent virgins to inebriated would-be murderers. As a result, though Miranda's words are to some extent undercut by irony, it is not too much of a stretch to think that Shakespeare really does mean this benediction on a world "[t]hat has such people in't!" After all, Prospero is another stand-in for the playwright, and he forgives all the wrongdoers at the end of the play. There is an element in the conclusion of The Tempest that celebrates the multiplicity and variety of human life, which, while it may result in complication and ambiguity, also creates humor, surprise, and love.

If The Tempest is read, as it often is, as a celebration of creativity and art, the aging Shakespeare's swan song to the theater, then this closing benediction may have a much broader application than just to this play, referring to the breadth of humanity that inspired the breadth of Shakespeare's characters. Similarly, Prospero's final request for applause in the monologue functions as a request for forgiveness, not merely for the wrongs he has committed in this play. It also requests forgiveness for the beneficent tyranny of creativity itself, in which an author, like a Prospero, moves people at his will, controls the minds of others, creates situations to suit his aims, and arranges outcomes entirely in the service of his own idea of goodness or justice or beauty. In this way, the ambiguity surrounding Prospero's power in The Tempest may be inherent to art itself. Like Prospero, authors work according to their own conceptions of a desirable or justifiable outcome. But as in The Tempest, a happy ending can restore harmony, and a well-developed play can create an authentic justice, even if it originates entirely in the mind of the author.

The plot of The Tempest is organized around the idea of persuasion, as Prospero gradually moves his sense of justice from his own mind into the outside world, gradually applying it to everyone around him until the audience believes it, too. This aggressive persuasiveness makes Prospero difficult to admire at times. Still, in another sense, persuasion characterizes the entire play, which seeks to enthrall audiences with its words and magic as surely as Prospero sought to enthrall Ariel. And because the audience decides whether it believes in the play—whether to applaud, as Prospero asks them to do—the real power lies not with the playwright, but with the viewer, not with the imagination that creates the story, but with the imagination that receives it. In this way, Shakespeare transforms the troubling ambiguity of the play into a surprising cause for celebration. The power wielded by Prospero, which seemed unsettling at first, is actually the source of all of our pleasure in the drama. In fact, it is the reason we came to the theater in the first place.

IMPORTANT QUOTATIONS EXPLAINED

1. You taught me language, and my profit on't
   Is I know how to curse. The red plague rid you
   For learning me your language! (I.ii.366–368)

This speech, delivered by Caliban to Prospero and Miranda, makes clear in a very concise form the vexed relationship between the colonized and the colonizer that lies at the heart of this play. The son of a witch, perhaps half-man and half-monster, his name a near-anagram of "cannibal," Caliban is an archetypal "savage" figure in a play that is much concerned with colonization and the controlling of wild environments. Caliban and Prospero have different narratives to explain their current relationship. Caliban sees Prospero as purely oppressive while Prospero claims that he has cared for and educated Caliban, or did until Caliban tried to rape Miranda. Prospero's narrative is one in which Caliban remains ungrateful for the help and civilization he has received from the Milanese Duke. Language, for Prospero and Miranda, is a means to knowing oneself, and Caliban has in their view shown nothing but scorn for this precious gift. Self-knowledge for Caliban, however, is not empowering. It is only a constant reminder of how he is different from Miranda and Prospero and how they have changed him from what he was. Caliban's only hope for an identity separate from those who have invaded his home is to use what they have given him against them.

2. There be some sports are painful, and their labour
    Delight in them sets off. Some kinds of baseness
    Are nobly undergone, and most poor matters
    Point to rich ends. This my mean task
    Would be as heavy to me as odious, but
    The mistress which I serve quickens what's dead
    And makes my labours pleasures. (III.i.1-7)

Ferdinand speaks these words to Miranda, as he expresses his willingness to perform the task Prospero has set him to, for her sake. *The Tempest* is very much about compromise and balance. Prospero must spend twelve years on an island in order to regain his dukedom; Alonso must seem to lose his son in order to be forgiven for his treachery; Ariel must serve Prospero in order to be set free; and Ferdinand must suffer Prospero's feigned wrath in order to reap true joy from his love for Miranda. This latter compromise is the subject of this passage from Act III, scene i, and we see the desire for balance expressed in the structure of Ferdinand's speech. This desire is built upon a series of antitheses—related but opposing ideas: "sports . . . painful" is followed by "labour . . . delights"; "baseness" can be undergone "nobly"; "poor matters" lead to "rich ends"; Miranda "quickens" (makes alive) what is "dead" in Ferdinand. Perhaps more than any other character in the play, Ferdinand is resigned to allow fate to take its course, always believing that the good will balance the bad in the end. His waiting for Miranda mirrors Prospero's waiting for reconciliation with his enemies, and it is probably Ferdinand's balanced outlook that makes him such a sympathetic character, even though we actually see or hear very little of him on-stage.

3. [I weep] at mine unworthiness, that dare not offer
    What I desire to give, and much less take
    What I shall die to want. But this is trifling,
    And all the more it seeks to hide itself
    The bigger bulk it shows. Hence, bashful cunning,
    And prompt me, plain and holy innocence.
    I am your wife, if you will marry me.
    If not, I'll die your maid. To be your fellow
    You may deny me, but I'll be your servant
    Whether you will or no (III.i.77–86)

Miranda delivers this speech to Ferdinand in Act III, scene i, declaring her undying love for him. Remarkably, she does not merely *propose* marriage, she practically insists upon it. This is one of two times in the play that Miranda seems to break out of the predictable character she has developed under the influence of her father's magic. The first time is in Act I, scene ii, when she scolds Caliban for his ingratitude to her after all the time she has spent teaching him to speak. In the speech quoted above, as in Act I, scene ii, Miranda seems to come to a point at which she can no longer hold inside what she thinks. It is not that her desires get the better of her; rather, she realizes the necessity of expressing her desires. The naïve girl who can barely hold still long enough to hear her father's long story in Act I, scene ii, and who is charmed asleep and awake as though she were a puppet, is replaced by a stronger, more mature individual at this moment. This speech, in which Miranda declares her sexual independence, using a metaphor that suggests both an erection and pregnancy (the "bigger bulk" trying to hide itself), seems to transform Miranda all at once from a girl into a woman.

At the same time, the last three lines somewhat undercut the power of this speech: Miranda seems, to a certain extent, a slave to her desires. Her pledge to follow Ferdinand, no matter what the cost to herself or what he desires, is echoed in the most degrading way possible by Caliban as he abases himself before the liquor-bearing Stefano. Ultimately, we know that Ferdinand and Miranda are right for one another from the fact that Ferdinand does not abuse the enormous trust Miranda puts in him.

4.   Be not afeard. The isle is full of noises,
       Sounds, and sweet airs, that give delight and hurt not.
       Sometimes a thousand twangling instruments
       Will hum about mine ears, and sometime voices
       That, if I then had waked after long sleep
       Will make me sleep again; and then in dreaming
       The clouds methought would open and show riches
       Ready to drop upon me, that when I waked
       I cried to dream again (III.ii.130–138).

This speech is Caliban's explanation to Stefano and Trinculo of mysterious music that they hear by magic. Though he claims that the chief virtue of his newly learned language is that it allows him to curse, Caliban here shows himself capable of using speech in a most sensitive and beautiful fashion. This speech is generally considered to be one of the most poetic in the play, and it is remarkable that Shakespeare chose to put it in the mouth of the drunken man-monster. Just when Caliban seems to have debased himself completely and to have become a purely ridiculous figure, Shakespeare gives him this speech and reminds the audience that Caliban has something within himself that Prospero, Stefano, Trinculo, and the audience itself generally cannot, or refuse to, see. It is unclear whether the "noises" Caliban discusses are the noises of the island itself or noises, like the music of the invisible Ariel, that are a result of Prospero's magic. Caliban himself does not seem to know where these noises come from. Thus his speech conveys the wondrous beauty of the island and the depth of his attachment to it, as well as a certain amount of respect and love for Prospero's magic, and for the possibility that he creates the "[s]ounds and sweet airs that give delight and hurt not."

QUOTATIONS

5.   Our revels now are ended. These our actors,
       As I foretold you, were all spirits, and
       Are melted into air, into thin air;
       And, like the baseless fabric of this vision,
       The cloud-capped towers, the gorgeous palaces,
       The solemn temples, the great globe itself,
       Yea, all which it inherit, shall dissolve;
       And, like this insubstantial pageant faded,
       Leave not a rack behind. We are such stuff
       As dreams are made on, and our little life
       Is rounded with a sleep. (IV.i.148–158)

Prospero speaks these lines just after he has remembers the plot against his life and sends the wedding masque away in order to deal with that plot. The sadness in the tone of the speech seems to be related to Prospero's surprising forgetfulness at this crucial moment in the play: he is so swept up in his own visions, in the power of his own magic, that for a moment he forgets the business of real life. From this point on, Prospero talks repeatedly of the "end" of his "labours" (IV.i.260), and of breaking his staff and drowning his magic book (V.i.54–57). One of Prospero's goals in bringing his former enemies to the island seems to be to extricate himself from a position of near absolute power, where the concerns of real life have not affected him. He looks forward to returning to Milan, where "every third thought shall be my grave" (V.i.315). In addition, it is with a sense of relief that he announces in the epilogue that he has given up his magic powers. Prospero's speech in Act IV, scene i emphasizes both the beauty of the world he has created for himself and the sadness of the fact that this world is in many ways meaningless because it is a kind of dream completely removed from anything substantial.

His mention of the "great globe," which to an audience in 1611 would certainly suggest the Globe Theatre, calls attention to Prospero's theatricality—to the way in which he controls events like a director or a playwright. The word "rack," which literally means "a wisp of smoke" is probably a pun on the "wrack," or shipwreck, with which the play began. These puns conflate the theatre and Prospero's island. When Prospero gives up his magic, the play will end, and the audience, like Prospero, will return to real life. No trace of the magical island will be left behind, not even of the shipwreck, for even the shipwreck was only an illusion.

KEY FACTS

FULL TITLE
   The Tempest

AUTHOR
   William Shakespeare

TYPE OF WORK
   Play

GENRE
   Romance

LANGUAGE
   Elizabethan English

TIME AND PLACE WRITTEN
   1610–1611; England

DATE OF FIRST PUBLICATION
   1623

PUBLISHER
   Isaac Jaggard and Edward Blount

TONE
   Dreamy, mysterious, magical

SETTING (TIME)
   The Renaissance

SETTING (PLACE)
   An island in the Mediterranean sea, probably off the coast
   of Italy

PROTAGONIST
   Prospero

MAJOR CONFLICT
   Prospero, the duke of Milan and a powerful magician, was
   banished from Italy and cast to sea by his usurping brother,
   Antonio, and Alonso, the king of Naples. As the play begins,
   Antonio and Alonso come under Prospero's magic power as they

sail past his island. Prospero seeks to use his magic to make these lords repent and restore him to his rightful place.

RISING ACTION

Prospero creates the tempest, causing his enemies' ship to wreck and its passengers to be dispersed about the island.

CLIMAX

Alonso and his party stop to rest, and Prospero causes a banquet to be set out before them. Just as they are about to eat, Ariel appears in the shape of a harpy and accuses them of their treachery against Prospero. Alonso is overwhelmed with remorse.

FALLING ACTION

Prospero brings Alonso and the others before him and forgives them. Prospero invites Alonso and his company to stay the night before everyone returns to Italy the next day, where Prospero will reassume his dukedom.

THEMES

The illusion of justice, the difficulty of distinguishing "men" from "monsters," the allure of ruling a colony

MOTIFS

Masters and servants, water and drowning, mysterious noises

SYMBOLS

The tempest, the game of chess, Prospero's books

FORESHADOWING

Prospero frequently hints at his plans to bring his enemies before him and to confront them for their treachery. Prospero also hints at his plans to relinquish his magic once he has confronted and forgiven his enemies.

STUDY QUESTIONS &
ESSAY TOPICS

STUDY QUESTIONS

1. *Analyze Caliban's "the isle is full of noises" speech (III.ii.130–138). What makes it such a compelling and beautiful passage? What is its relation to Caliban's other speeches, and to his character in general? What effect does this speech have on our perception of Caliban's character? Why does Shakespeare give these lines to Caliban rather than, say, Ariel or Miranda?*

Caliban's speech is most remarkable and compelling largely because of how different it is from anything he has said before. Caliban frequently describes the qualities of the island, but usually these descriptions relate to the torments Prospero subjects him to. Indeed, the speech in Act III, scene ii echoes one from the beginning of Act II, scene ii, in which Caliban complains of the spirits that Prospero has sent to bother him. Like the earlier speech, the speech in Act III, scene ii repeats the word "sometime" twice, and like the earlier speech it seems to discuss the workings of spirits on the island. Unlike the earlier speech, however, the speech in Act III, scene ii takes us into a hypnotic dream world, where there seems to be a magic greater than Prospero's. The voices Caliban hears do not command him to work, but rather, if they wake him from sleep, put him back to sleep again. In Caliban's speech, even the rain is transformed. The words "The clouds methought would open" suggests an image of rain, but what Caliban imagines is "riches / Ready to drop upon me" (II.ii.136–137). The harsh, tangible things of this island—Prospero's voice, the pinches of spirits, the weather—become in this speech beautiful noises, possibly only dreams, that "give delight and hurt not" (II.ii.131).

Caliban is drunk when he gives this speech, and while it certainly brings the audience to rapt attention, the speech does not do much to change Caliban's character. He continues to range drunkenly about the island with Trinculo and Stefano. What the speech does is

57

change our perception of Caliban. It reveals a deeply tragic side of him. His life on the island is so terrible that he longs for the ethereal world of the noises that give him delight. In the mouth of Miranda, or Ariel, this speech might be just as beautiful, and would convey effectively the magic of the island. But it has more power in Caliban because it allows his curses and his drunkenness to make tragic sense: since the arrival of Prospero, the island's beauty is no longer Caliban's.

2.   *What is the nature of Prospero and Miranda's relationship? Discuss moments where Miranda seems to be entirely dependent on her father and moments where she seems independent. How does Miranda's character change over the course of the play?*

At first, Miranda seems very young. When Prospero tells her of his exile from Italy, it is her passionate but also restless youth that the reader sees in her exclamations of concern ("O the heavens!" I.ii.116; "Alack, for pity!" I.ii.132). In this scene the reader sees a relationship that is tender but also astonishingly one-sided. Prospero has lived alone with his daughter for twelve years and not told her why they live alone on the island. After he has told her, he charms her to sleep so that he can set about the new plan of getting her a husband, which he has not discussed with her. When that future husband, Ferdinand, arrives, Prospero continues to dominate her by directing her gaze toward Ferdinand, but then quickly steps between the two. When Miranda begs him to have mercy upon Ferdinand, Prospero is strikingly harsh.

Prospero's love for Miranda is most evident in his willingness to remain quiet while Miranda talks to Ferdinand in Act III, scene i. Though Prospero enters, unseen, at the same time as Miranda in this scene, he does not say a word until she and Ferdinand have left the stage. During that time, Miranda remembers that her father has given her "precepts" (III.i.58) against talking with Ferdinand—and then breaks them by trusting her desires and proposing marriage to him (III.i.77–86). By the end of the scene, Miranda seems almost to have forgotten her father entirely, and she seems much older, in control of her destiny. By leaving her alone for perhaps the first time, Prospero has allowed Miranda to leave behind her childhood. The transition is not complete, however, and may not become complete, even by the end of the play. In Act IV, scene i, Miranda speaks only two and a half lines, standing completely silent while her father and

Ferdinand discuss the details of her marriage. And while Miranda speaks first, and forthrightly, when she appears in Act V, scene i, she appears only after being revealed behind a curtain by her father. Her final lines, "O brave new world / That has such people in't" (V.i.186–187) while gloriously hopeful, are also painfully ironic. The isolation her life has forced upon her has made her mistake for "brave" a cast of characters that the audience knows only too well to be deeply flawed.

3. *Discuss Ferdinand's character. What is the nature of his love for Miranda? Is he a likable character? What is the nature of his relationship to other characters?*

Ferdinand is very formal. Upon first seeing Miranda, he assumes that she is a goddess, and he addresses her as such. His language is that of courtly love, of knights who fight for fair ladies. Ferdinand idealizes both Miranda and love itself. From the moment he sees her, he is intent upon finding himself in a heaven of love.

While Ferdinand's formality is in some ways endearing, it is also in some ways disturbingly reminiscent of Prospero. Some of Ferdinand's long speeches, especially the speech about Miranda's virginity in Act IV, scene i, sound quite similar to the way Prospero speaks. Ferdinand is a sympathetic character, and his love for Miranda seems most genuine when he suddenly is able to break out of his verbose formality and show a strikingly simple interest in Miranda. The reader can see this when he asks Miranda, "What is your name?" (III.i.36). The reader notices it again in Act V, scene i when he jests with her over a game of chess, and when he tells his father, who asks whether Miranda is "the goddess that hath severed us, / And brought us together," that "she is mortal" (V.i.190–191). Ferdinand agrees to marry Miranda in a scene in which he has been, like Caliban, hauling logs for Prospero. Unlike Caliban, however, Ferdinand has been carrying wood gladly, believing that he serves Miranda. The sweet humbleness implicit in this belief seems to shine through best at the times when Ferdinand lets go of his romantic language.

Suggested Essay Topics

1. Discuss one or more of the play's comic scenes involving
    Trinculo, Stefano, and Caliban. How do these scenes parallel
    and parody the main action of the play? Pay particular
    attention to Trinculo's speech about Caliban in Act II, scene ii,
    lines 18–38. This is one of the longest speeches in the play.
    How does it relate to larger thematic issues in the play, such as
    the difference between "men" and "monsters," or the
    relationship between colonizers and the colonized?

2. Look at a few of the many passages in the play in which there
    is mention of noises, sound, or music. Focusing on one or two
    characters, discuss the role of noise in THE TEMPEST.

3. Virtually every character in the play expresses some desire to
    be lord of the island. Discuss two or three of these characters.
    How does each envision the island's potential? How does each
    envision his own rule?

4. Analyze the tempest scene in Act I, scene i. Topics to discuss
    include the following. How does Shakespeare use the very
    limited resources of his bare stage to create a sense of realism?
    How are we introduced to the characters? How does this
    introduction affect our perception of them later? How does
    the dialogue of this scene relate to the content or themes of the
    rest of the play? How is this scene echoed in later parts of the
    play?

Review & Resources

Quiz

1. Whom does Caliban mistake for one of Prospero's spirits sent to torment him?

   A. Stefano
   B. Ferdinand
   C. Miranda
   D. Trinculo

2. What was Prospero's title before his position was usurped and he was forced to flee Italy?

   A. Duke of Milan
   B. King of Naples
   C. Duke of Naples
   D. Pope of Rome

3. From which country is Alonso's ship returning when it is caught in the tempest?

   A. Naples
   B. England ·
   C. Tunis
   D. Bermudas

4. How long have Prospero and Miranda been on their island?

   A. Ten years
   B. Fifteen years
   C. Twelve years
   D. One day

5. What was the name of Caliban's mother?

   A. Ariel
   B. Claribel
   C. Sycorax
   D. Setebos

6. Over how many days does the action of The Tempest take place?

   A. Two
   B. One
   C. Three
   D. Four

7. Which mythical figures appear in the wedding masque Prospero stages for Miranda and Ferdinand?

   A. Cupid, Venus, and Mars
   B. Jupiter and Saturn
   C. Ceres, Iris, and Juno
   D. Isis and Osiris

8. Which character is Prospero's brother?

   A. Alonso
   B. Sebastian
   C. Gonzalo
   D. Antonio

9. Which character is Sebastian's brother?

   A. Prospero
   B. Antonio
   C. Gonzalo
   D. Alonso

10. What do we see Miranda and Ferdinand doing in the play's final scene?

    A. Playing cards
    B. Carrying wood
    C. Playing chess
    D. Playing tag

11. What shape does Ariel assume at the magical banquet in Act III, scene iii?

   A. Harpy
   B. Eagle
   C. Sea-nymph
   D. Hound

12. What do Prospero and Ariel set out as bait for Caliban, Trinculo, and Stefano?

   A. "a butt of sack"
   B. "the nimble marmoset"
   C. "glistening apparel"
   D. "a thousand twangling instruments"

13. What does Caliban say must be done before Prospero can be killed?

   A. His magic cloak must be burnt
   B. His books must be seized
   C. Miranda must be killed
   D. A tempest must be raised

14. What is the name of Alonso's daughter?

   A. Claribel
   B. Miranda
   C. Sycorax
   D. Alonsa

15. What does Prospero give as his reason for treating Caliban badly?

   A. Caliban tried to kill him
   B. Caliban tried to steal his books
   C. Caliban is merely a beast
   D. Caliban attempted to rape Miranda

REVIEW & RESOURCES

16.   Who helped Prospero and Miranda to flee Italy?

    A.   Antonio
    B.   Gonzalo
    C.   Trinculo
    D.   Claribel

17.   Where does Ariel put the mariners and Boatswain after the tempest?

    A.   In a thicket
    B.   Under Caliban's cloak
    C.   Asleep in the ship in the harbor
    D.   In Prospero's cell

18.   Where did Sycorax imprison Ariel?

    A.   On another island
    B.   In a cloven pine
    C.   In a lion's den
    D.   Inside a stone

19.   What task are both Caliban and Ferdinand forced to perform?

    A.   Marrying Miranda
    B.   Singing drunkenly
    C.   Collecting berries
    D.   Carrying wood

20.   Who persuades Sebastian to try to kill Alonso?

    A.   Antonio
    B.   Gonzalo
    C.   Ariel
    D.   Alonso

21.   What does Prospero intend to "drown" after he has reconciled with his enemies?

    A.   His magic garments
    B.   His book
    C.   His staff
    D.   Caliban

REVIEW & RESOURCES

22. What does Caliban say is his "chief profit" from learning language?

    A. He knows how to curse
    B. He can show Prospero the "qualities o' th' isle"
    C. He can woo Miranda
    D. He can sing with Trinculo and Stefano

23. Which characters do Stefano and Trinculo most clearly parody?

    A. Prospero and Miranda
    B. Caliban and Sycorax
    C. Alonso and Gonzalo
    D. Antonio and Sebastian

24. What is the final task Prospero orders Ariel to perform?

    A. To release Sycorax
    B. To haul a load of wood
    C. To give the fleet calm seas on its return to Italy
    D. To take charge of Caliban

25. We are told that one of the following characters has visited England. Which one?

    A. Stefano
    B. Prospero
    C. Trinculo
    D. Alonso

SUGGESTIONS FOR FURTHER READING

BRADBROOK, MURIEL. *Themes and Conventions in Elizabethan Drama.* Cambridge: Cambridge University Press, 1960.

GRAFF, GERALD, and JAMES PHELAN, eds. The Tempest: *A Case Study in Critical Controversy.* Boston: Bedford/St. Martin's, 2000.

GURR, ANDREW. *The Shakespearean Stage, 1574-1642.* Cambridge: Cambridge University Press, 1992.

MURPHY, PATRICK M., ed. The Tempest: *Critical Essays.* New York: Garland, 2000.

PALMER, D., ed. *Shakespeare:* The Tempest: *A Casebook.* Nashville: Aurora Publishers, 1970.

RICHARDS, JENNIFER, and JAMES KNOWLES, eds. *Shakespeare's Late Plays: New Readings.* Edinburgh: Edinburgh University Press, 1999.

SMITH, HALLETT DARIUS, ed. The Tempest: *A Collection of Critical Essays.* Englewood Cliffs, New Jersey: Prentice-Hall, 1969.

VAUGHAN, VIRGINIA MASON, and ALDEN T. VAUGHAN, eds. *Critical Essays on Shakespeare's* The Tempest. New York: G. K. Hall, 1998.